SPEAKING UP AT WORK

SPEAKING UP AT WORK

The International Institute of Minnesota
Catherine Robinson and Jenise Rowekamp

Oxford University Press

Oxford University Press

198 Madison Avenue, New York, NY 10016 USA

Great Clarendon Street, Oxford OX2 6DP England

Oxford New York
Athens Auckland Bangkok Bogotá Buenos Aires
Cape Town Chennai Dar es Salaam Delhi Florence Hong Kong Istanbul
Karachi Kolkata Kuala Lumpur Madrid Melbourne Mexico City Mumbai
Nairobi Paris São Paulo Shanghai Singapore Taipei Tokyo Toronto Warsaw

and associated companies in
Berlin Ibadan

OXFORD is a trademark of Oxford University Press.

ISBN 0-19-434196-8

Illustrations by Beth Upton and Susan Maher.

Photographs by Simon Baigelman.

Cover photograph by Halley Ganges.

Cover design by Karen Siegel.

The publishers are grateful to Group Health, Inc., for permission to reproduce the form on page 135.

Printing (last digit): 20 19 18 17 16 15 14 13 12

Printed in Hong Kong

Table of Contents

Contents

Acknowledgments

This publication was developed as an Education Department project of the International Institute of Minnesota, an affiliate of the American Council for Nationalities Service. Major funding for the project was received from the Minnesota Refugee Program Office/Office of Refugee Resettlement, Ramsey County Commissioners, and the F. R. Bigelow Foundation.

The authors wish to thank Kevin O'Neil and Margaret Wilke of Literacy 85. Their employment survey, which identified problems that workers with limited English proficiency were having in the workplace, was an invaluable source in the writing of these materials. Bibliographical information, including this survey and a list of other references that were helpful in preparing this text, appear in the *Teacher's Manual*.

Finally, we would like to thank the many professionals who took the time to review the draft of these materials and who offered many useful suggestions. We are especially grateful to Susan Lanzano of Oxford University Press for her editorial guidance.

C.R.
J.R.

Preface

This competency-based textbook was written to help adults with limited English proficiency be successful employees. One of the biggest challenges in writing these materials was getting close to the workplace of these workers in order to assess their needs. To better understand workers' problems, the authors visited various job sites and spoke to counselors at employment projects. One of the most useful sources of information was a survey done by Literacy 85 (St. Paul, Minnesota) in which employers and supervisors identified problems that limited English proficiency workers experience in the workplace. The information gained from these sources made it clear that these workers not only need skills which will help them obtain employment, but—perhaps more importantly—skills which will help them maintain employment and advance on the job. It is these last two areas of need which are addressed in *Speaking Up at Work*.

While *Speaking Up at Work* was developed with the non-native speaker in mind, it has been found to be equally valuable for native-speaking youth and young adults who need employment readiness skills.

The book consists of eleven units, each of which is divided into three sections. The first section deals with cultural information and language for improving social interaction. The second section is concerned with language and culture for learning the job and for increasing worker flexibility. The emphasis in these two sections is on oral communication. The final section in each unit presents information to help workers understand job policies and procedures.

To give equal representation to males and females throughout and avoid the clumsiness of using double pronouns every time we refer to an unspecified person, we have generally used male and female pronouns in alternation. However, when making reference to people who in the students' lives are real, such as teachers or spouses, we have used the double pronoun so that the reference makes sense to them.

1

Greeting and Addressing People

Conversation 1

Paul sees his friend Sam before work.

Paul: Morning, Sam. How're you doing?
Sam: Pretty good. And you?
Paul: Not bad. How's the work going?
Sam: Good.
Paul: See you at lunch.
Sam: Okay. See you later.

Conversation 2

On his way out of work, Sam sees his boss, Mr. Jones.

Mr. Jones: Hello, Sam.
Sam: Hello, Mr. Jones.
Mr. Jones: How's your family?
Sam: Excuse me?
Mr. Jones: How is your family?
Sam: Oh, they're fine, thanks.
Mr. Jones: Have a nice evening, Sam.
Sam: You, too, Mr. Jones.

Write T for true and F for false.

_____ 1. Paul and Sam are friends.

_____ 2. Paul will see Sam at lunch.

_____ 3. Mr. Jones is Sam's boss.

_____ 4. Sam understands everything Mr. Jones says.

_____ 5. *How are you doing?* means *How are you?*

Useful Expressions

1. Addressing people using titles

Mr. Jones   men (any marital status)
Ms. Smith   women (any marital status)
Mrs. Diaz   married women only
Miss Lee   single women only

Note: *Mr., Ms., Mrs.,* and *Miss* are only used with last names (family names).

Practice

With which people would you be formal and use titles? Circle your answers.

1. a close friend
2. your lead worker
3. a new teacher
4. your boss

5. a worker you don't know well
6. your manager
7. a man interviewing you
8. the principal at your child's school

2. Greeting people formally

- ■ Good morning, Mr. Jones,
   How are you?
- □ I'm fine, thank you. And you?
- ■ I'm fine, thanks.

- ■ Hello, Mrs. Diaz.
   How are you?
- □ I'm fine, thanks. And you?
- ■ I'm fine, thank you.

Practice

Find out the last names of the people in your class and practice conversations like the ones above.

3. Greeting people informally

- ■ Morning, Jim. How're you doing?
- □ Pretty good, How about you?
- ■ Not bad, thanks.

- ■ Hi, Maria, How's it going?
- □ Not bad. And you?
- ■ Pretty good, thanks.

Practice

Find out the first names of people in your class and practice conversations like the ones above.

4. Asking about someone's job or family

■ How's your *job?*
□ It's fine, thanks.

■ How're your *children?*
□ They're fine, thank you.

Practice

Practice the conversation with a partner. Substitute a different word each time.

1. wife
2. family
3. son
4. daughter

5. husband
6. kids
7. sons
8. daughters

5. Asking for repetition

■ Excuse me?
Pardon me?
(I'm sorry.) What was that?
(Excuse me.) What was that?

Practice

Practice getting something repeated that you didn't hear or understand.

Examples:

job
■ How's your *job?*
□ I'm sorry. What was that?
■ How is your *job?*
□ It's fine, thanks.

children
■ How are your *children?*
□ I'm sorry. What was that?
■ How are your *children?*
□ They're fine, thanks.

1. wife
2. family
3. son
4. daughter

5. husband
6. kids
7. sons
8. daughters

6. Saying good-bye

■ See you later.
□ Good-bye.

■ Bye.
□ See you tomorrow.

■ See you at lunch.
□ Okay. See you later.

■ Nice talking to you.
□ Same here.

■ Have a nice evening.
□ You too.

Practice

Practice saying good-bye to your partner. The first time be each other's friends. The second time be boss and worker.

Friend 1: Bye, Ana.
Friend 2: See you tomorrow, Mee.

Worker: Good-bye, Mr. Vang.
Boss: Have a nice evening, Ana.

Role-plays

Boss

1. You greet a worker coming into work in the morning. You ask him how he is and how his family is.

Worker

You see your boss before work in the morning. You ask her to repeat something you didn't hear. You tell your boss to have a nice day.

Friend

2. It's after work in the afternoon. You say hello to your friend and ask how he is.

Friend

You ask how your friend's work is going. You tell your friend to have a nice evening.

For role-plays 3 and 4, get into groups of four. You are a worker. Another student is your boss; another is your lead worker; and the other is your friend.

3. You are starting work in the morning. Greet each of these people and ask how they are: your boss, your lead worker, and your friend.

4. You are leaving work. Say good-bye to each of these people before you go: your boss, your lead worker, and your friend.

In the U.S.

Read the following paragraph. Then circle what you think is the best answer.

Vone is a very hard worker. She is always on time. She comes to work and goes right to her desk without speaking to anyone. When people say hello to her, she speaks very softly and doesn't look at the person. She never asks other people how they are. What do people think of Vone?

a. They think she's shy.

b. They think she's rude and unfriendly.

c. They think she's a hard worker and doesn't have time to talk.

Using What You've Learned

At work this week, try to greet someone in English every day. Ask the person who he is or how his family or work is. Tell your class whom you spoke to and what you said.

Asking for Clarification

Conversation

The teacher is helping Shoua fill out the registration card for his evening class.

Teacher: On the first line, I want you to print your last name and then your first name.

Shoua: Last name, first name?

Teacher: Right. On the second line, I want your street address, city, state, and zip code.

Shoua: Could you repeat line two again?

Teacher: Sure. Write your address, city, state, and zip code.

Shoua: Okay.

Teacher: On the third line, write your native country.

Shoua: I'm sorry. I don't understand that.

Teacher: I want to know where you are from.

Shoua: Oh, I see.

Teacher: Good. Now on line four, put how many years you've studied English. Do you understand that?

Shoua: Yes, I understand. I studied three months in Thailand and one year in the States.

Teacher: Well, that's it.

Shoua: (completes registration card and shows it to teacher) Is this correct?

Teacher: Yes, it's fine.

Write T for true or F for false.

_____ 1. Shoua understands everything.

_____ 2. Shoua asks questions when he doesn't understand.

_____ 3. Shoua's teacher is happy to explain things to him.

_____ 4. Shoua didn't understand the words *native country*.

Useful Expressions

1. Asking to have instructions repeated

■ Please repeat that.
I'm sorry. I don't understand that.

| Could you please | say that more slowly? |
| | explain *native country?* |

2. Saying that you understand

■ Okay.
(Okay.) Now I understand.
Oh, I see.

Practice

Practice getting something repeated and then tell your partner that you understand. Substitute a new word each time.

Example: *name*

■ Write your *name.*   1. first name
□ Could you repeat that?   2. city and state
■ Write your *name.*   3. address
□ Okay.   4. zip code

3. Checking that you understand

■ Write your last name and then your first name.
□ Last name, first name?
■ Right.

■ Turn to Unit 1, Section Three.
□ Section Three?
■ Right.

Practice

Practice conversations like the ones above.

Example:
■ *Write your address and your zip code.*
□ Address and zip code?
■ Right.

1. Turn to page 165.
2. Write the date in the top right hand corner.
3. Open your book to Unit 1, Section Three.
4. Write your first name and then your last name.
5. My zip code is 55102.

4. Confirming understanding

■ Do you	understand?		□ Yes, I	do.
	get it?			understand.
			No, I	don't.
				don't get it.
				don't understand.

■ Do you have any questions?		□ No,	I don't.
Any questions?			no questions.
			I understand.
			I get it.
		Yes, I	do.
			have a question.
			have a few questions.

8

Practice

Look at the picture and answer the questions.

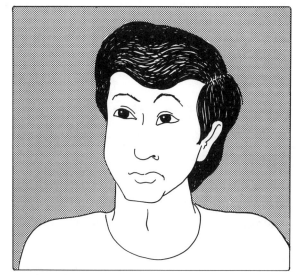

Example: ■ Do you understand?

☐ Yes, I do.

1. ■ Any questions?

☐ . . . .

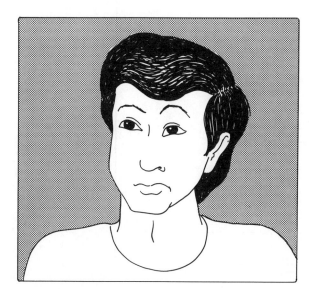

2. ■ Do you get it?

☐ . . . .

3. ■ Do you have any questions?

☐ . . . .

5. Getting your work checked

■ Is this	right?		☐ Yes,	it's fine.
	correct?			very good.
	okay?			that's it.
			No,	it isn't.

Practice

Practice conversations like this with your partner.

■ Write your name.
□ Is this right?
■ Yes, very good.

Training Exercise

Note to the teacher: Complete instructions for leading this training exercise appear in the *Teacher's Manual.*

Note to the student: Listen to your teacher's instructions and fill out this registration card. If you don't understand something, ask your teacher to repeat. If you are not sure about something, check with your teacher.

REGISTRATION CARD

Personal information

1. _____ ☐

2. _____ _____

3. _____ _____

Education

4. _____ _____ _____

5. _____ years in _____

6. a. _____ in _____

    b. _____ in _____

Employment

7. yes no _____

8. yes no _____

    _____

9. yes no _____

_____ _____

In the U.S.

Read the following problem. Then circle what you think is the best answer.

Mary is at work. Her supervisor is helping her fill out her time card. She understands step one and step two, but she doesn't understand step three. What should she do?

a. Not say anything to her supervisor.

b. Ask her supervisor to explain step three again.

c. Ask a friend to help her tomorrow.

Understanding Work Schedules

	SUE	LEE	TOU	MAY	JO	BILL	PAT
M	✕	11-7	7-3	✕	11-7	3-11	✕
T	✕	11-7	7-3	✕	11-7	3-11	✕
W	?	✕	?	11-7	6-11	3-11	11-7
Th	?	✕	?	11-7			11-7
F	7-3	✕	?	?			-7
Sa	7-3	11-7	✕	3-11			
Su	6-11		7-3	3-11			

Work Schedule

Work Schedules

There are two kinds of work schedules.

1. Some tell you when you have to work.
2. Others tell you when you have to work and what you have to do.

In this section, you will learn to read and understand both kinds of schedules.

Practice

Study the work schedules on the next two pages, and then answer the questions.

Work Schedule 1

A-1 Welding Work Schedule

FOR FEB. 16-22, 1986

	Day Shift 8 a.m.-4 p.m.	**Swing Shift** 4 p.m.-12 mid.	**Graveyard Shift** 12 mid.-8 a.m.
Su	—	—	—
M	AMY	JEFF	SOM
T	JEFF	AMY	SOM
W	AMY	JEFF	SOM
Th	JEFF	AMY	SOM
F	AMY	JEFF	SOM
Sa	—	—	—

1. What week is this work schedule for? _____

2. Who works the same shift every day? _____

3. When does Jeff work the day shift? _____

4. How many days does Amy work the swing shift? _____

   What days are they? _____

5. Does any worker work two shifts in a row? _____

6. Does any worker work on Saturday or Sunday? _____

7. What time is the graveyard shift? _____

8. What shift does Amy work on Monday? _____

Work Schedule 2

JOHNSON'S JANITORIAL SERVICE
Work Schedule
FEB. 3-7 1986   SHIFT 4:00 P.M. – 12:00 MID.

NAME	(M)	(T)	(W)	(Th)	(F)
SHOUA XIONG	vacuum offices 101-105	general clean 101-105 →		windows 101-105 →	
TOM RUSSO	wax floors 1st floor →		wax floors 2nd floor →		wax floors lobby
LIZ BROWN	vacuum offices 201-205	general clean 201-205 →		windows 201-205 →	
KIM LONG	clean floors 2nd floor →		clean floors lobby	clean floors 3rd floor →	

1. What week is this work schedule for? _____

2. What shift do these workers have? _____

3. Do they work on Saturday and Sunday? _____

4. Do the workers do the same work every day? _____

5. What does Tom Russo have to do on Friday this week? _____

_____

6. How many days does Shoua Xiong have to clean windows? _____

_____

What days? _____ Where? _____

7. When does Liz do general cleaning? _____ Where? _____

_____

8. What does Kim have to do on Tuesday? _____

Using What You've Learned

A. Answer these questions about your workplace.

1. Does the work schedule at your workplace change sometimes? _____

   How often does it change? _____

2. When is the work schedule posted? _____

3. Where is it posted? _____

4. What information is on your work schedule? _____

B. If you are working, bring a current work schedule from your workplace to class and discuss it with your classmates.

Phoning in Sick

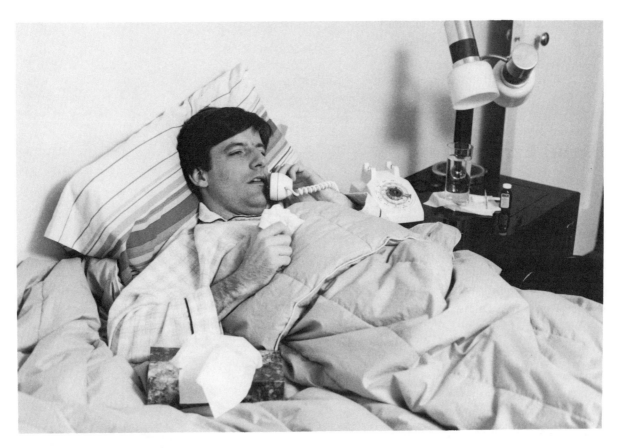

Conversation

It is 7:45 in the morning. Peter has the flu. His fever is 102°. He is calling his supervisor at work.

Secretary: Johnson's Cleaning Company. Can I help you?
Peter: May I speak to Mary Allen, please?
Secretary: Just a minute, please.

●●●

Mary: Hello. Mary Allen speaking.
Peter: Hello, Mary. This is Peter Watson.
Mary: Hello, Peter. What can I do for you?
Peter: Mary, I won't be in today.
Mary: What's the problem?

Peter: I have the flu.
Mary: That's too bad. Do you think you'll be in tomorrow?
Peter: Sorry. What was that?
Mary: Are you coming back tomorrow?
Peter: I hope so.
Mary: Okay. I hope you feel better.
Peter: Thanks. Good-bye.

Write T for true and F for false.

_____ 1. Peter is not going to work this morning.
_____ 2. Peter is calling work because he is going to be late this morning.
_____ 3. Peter speaks to the secretary first.
_____ 4. Mary is Peter's supervisor.
_____ 5. Peter has the flu.
_____ 6. Peter will not be in tomorrow.

Useful Expressions

1. Asking to speak to someone on the phone

■ International Institute. Can | I help you?
                           May |

□ I'd like to | speak | to Mary Allen, please.
              | talk |

■ Just a minute, | please.
  Can you hold, |

   ●●●

☑ Hello, Mary Allen speaking.
□ Hello, Mary. This is Peter Watson.
☑ Hi, Peter. What can I do for you?

Practice

Practice the above conversation with your partner.

2. Explaining absence from work

■ I can't come to	work today.	□ Why?	
	school today.	What's the	matter?
I won't be in today.			problem?

■ I'm sick.		□ That's too bad.
I have	the flu.	I'm sorry to hear it.
	a cold.	Sorry to hear it.

Practice

Practice this conversation with your partner. Change the excuse each time.

Example: *I'm sick.*

■ I won't be in today.
□ What's the matter?
■ *I'm sick.*
□ Sorry to hear it.

1. I have the flu.
2. My son is sick.
3. I broke my arm.

4. I have a bad cold.
5. _____
6. _____

3. Answering questions about returning to work

■ | Do you | be in tomorrow?
    think you'll |
    Will you |

□ | Yes, I hope so.
    I'm not sure.

■ When will you be | back?
                in?

□ | Tomorrow.
    Soon, I hope.

Practice 1

Practice conversations like these with your partner.

■ When will you be back?
□ Tomorrow, I hope.

■ Will you be in tomorrow?
□ I'm not sure.

Practice 2

Read this conversation with your partner and then fill in the missing lines. You want to speak to your teacher.

Secretary: International Institute. Can I help you?

Student: _____

Secretary: Just a minute, please.

Teacher: Hello, _____ speaking.
                     (your teacher's name)

Student: _____

Teacher: Hello, _____. What can I do for you?

Student: _____

Teacher: What's the problem?

Student: _____

Teacher: That's too bad. Do you think you'll be back tomorrow?

Student: _____

Teacher: Okay. I hope you feel better.

Student: _____

Teacher: Good-bye, _____

Role-plays

Your teacher will play the secretary/supervisor role.

1. You are sick. You have a fever of 102°. You are not sure when you can come back to work. You call your supervisor, Mr. Trang.

2. You broke your arm last night. Your arm is in a cast, but the doctor wants you to rest for two days before going back to work. You call your foreman, John Pappas.

3. Your child has a strep throat. She has to stay home for one day. You can't get a babysitter because the child is contagious until tomorrow. You call your boss, Ms. Allen.

In the U.S.

A. Read each problem. Then circle what you think is the best answer.

1. Alice woke up at 7:30 with a fever of 103°. She should be at work at 9:00. What should she do?

   a. Go back to sleep and call her supervisor at noon when she feels better.

   b. Get dressed and go to work even though she is sick.

   c. Call her supervisor as soon as work opens.

2. Stan missed work today because he was sick. He didn't call his supervisor because he was only going to miss one day. What does Stan's supervisor think about Stan's not calling?

   a. He thinks Stan is irresponsible.

   b. He's glad Stan didn't bother him about such a small problem.

   c. Stan's supervisor is sure he has a good reason for being absent.

B. Read the following reasons for being absent from work. If the reason is acceptable, write *OK*. If the reason is not acceptable, write *Not OK*.

_____ 1. You have the flu.

_____ 2. You are too tired.

_____ 3. Your car won't start.

_____ 4. You are moving today. You told your manager two weeks ago.

_____ 5. You broke your leg yesterday.

_____ 6. Your brother just arrived from Thailand and is staying at your house.

_____ 7. Your wife had a baby last night.

_____ 8. You have to go to your grandfather's funeral.

_____ 9. Your children are sick. Yesterday your wife stayed home with the children, but today she is going to work and you have to stay with the children.

_____ 10. You are going to go to a family meeting in another state. You will be gone a week, but you have used all your vacation days for this year.

Giving and Asking for Directions

Conversation 1

Ahmed just started work today. He and his friend Peter are working on the second floor in the shop.

Peter: There's the lunch bell.

Ahmed: You're right. Say, Peter, is the lunchroom on this floor?

Peter: No, it's downstairs. Go to the first floor. At the bottom of the stairs, turn right. Go to the end of the corridor and take a left. It's the first door on the left past the elevator.

Ahmed: Thanks, Peter.

FLOOR PLAN OF AHMED'S FACTORY   FIRST FLOOR

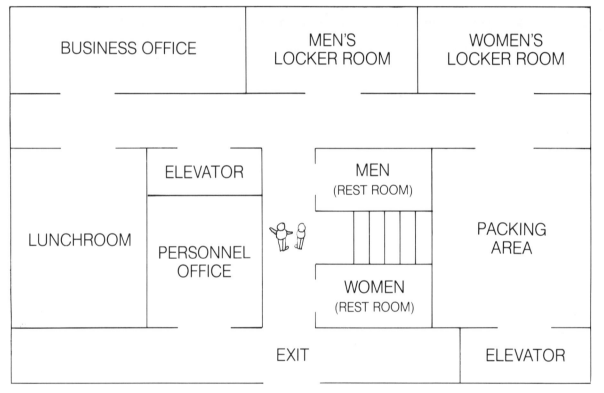

Ahmed goes downstairs, but he can't find the lunchroom.

Ahmed: Excuse me. Where's the lunchroom?

Worker: It's at the other end of the corridor on the left, across from the business office.

Ahmed: Thanks.

Write T for true and F for false.

_____ 1. Ahmed wants to go to the lunchroom.

_____ 2. The lunchroom is upstairs.

_____ 3. Ahmed asks two people where the lunchroom is.

_____ 4. The lunchroom is next to the business office.

SECOND FLOOR

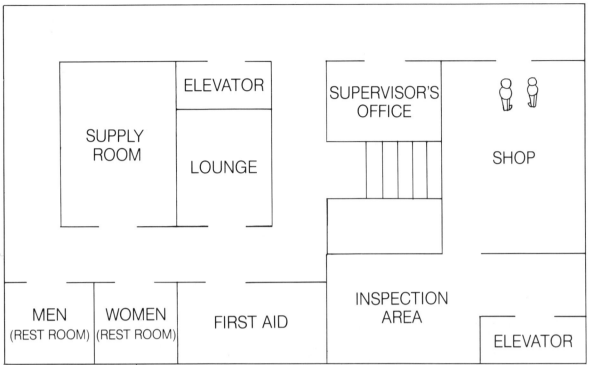

Conversation 2

Later in the afternoon, Ahmed is looking for the supply room.

Ahmed: Excuse me. Can you tell me how to get to the supply room?
Worker: Sure. Go out and turn left. Take a left at the first hall. Go to the end of the hall and turn right. It's the second door on the right.
Ahmed: Thanks.

Conversation 3

At the supply room.

Ahmed: Hi. I need some light bulbs.
Worker: They're on the top shelf of that cupboard.
Ahmed: Which shelf?
Worker: On the top shelf.
Ahmed: Thanks.
Worker: That's okay.

Write T for true and F for false.

_____ 1. In the afternoon, Ahmed is looking for the supply room.

_____ 2. Ahmed needs light bulbs.

_____ 3. The light bulbs are in a cupboard on the bottom shelf.

_____ 4. Ahmed finds the light bulbs himself.

Useful Expressions

1. Asking for directions

■ Excuse me. | Where's the lunchroom?
Can | you tell me where the lunchroom is?
Could |

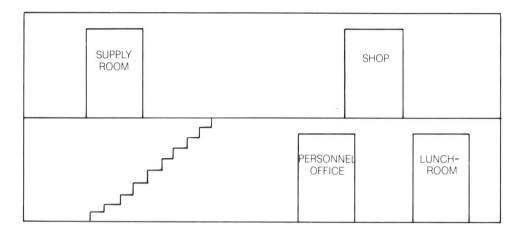

2. Giving directions (1)

■ | The supply room is upstairs.
The personnel office is downstairs.
The shop is on | the second floor.
| two.
Personnel is on | the first floor.
| one.
The lunchroom is next to personnel.

Practice

Look at the pictures and practice conversations like the example.

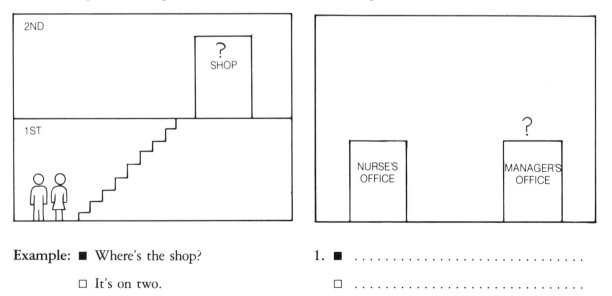

Example: ■ Where's the shop?

□ It's on two.

1. ■ . . . .

□ . . . .

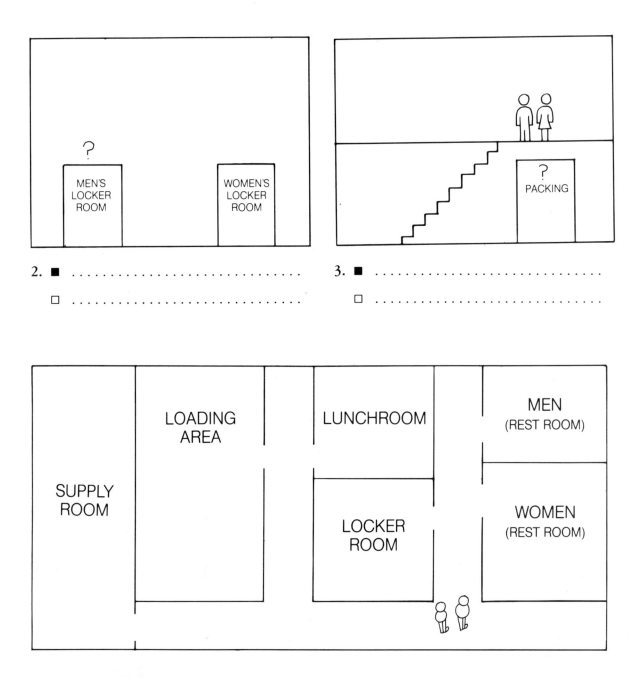

2. ■ . . . .

   □ . . . .

3. ■ . . . .

   □ . . . .

3. Giving directions (2)

■ | The locker room is the first door on the left.
The rest room is the second door on the right.
The loading area is across from the lunchroom.
The supply room is at the end of the | hall.
corridor.

Practice

Look at the pictures and practice conversations using the expressions above.

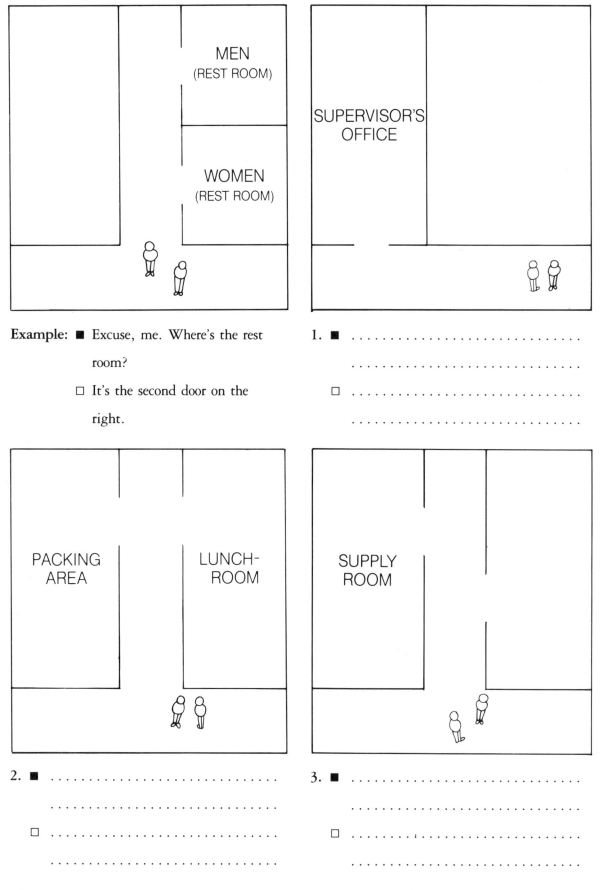

Example: ■ Excuse, me. Where's the rest room?

□ It's the second door on the right.

1. ■ ....
....
□ ....
....

2. ■ ....
....
□ ....
....

3. ■ ....
....
□ ....
....

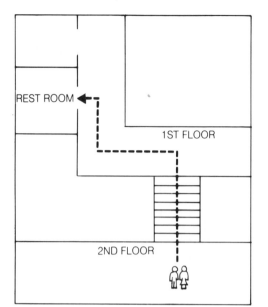

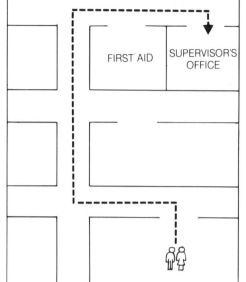

4. Giving directions (3)

■ Excuse me. Which way is the rest room?

□ Go downstairs. At the bottom of the stairs, turn left. Go to the end of the hall and turn right. It's the first door on the left.

■ Thanks.

■ Pardon me. How do I get to the supervisor's office?

□ Go out and turn left. At the first hall take a right and go straight. At the end of the hall, turn right and go past first aid. It's the second door on the right.

■ Thank you.

Practice 1

Note to the teacher: Instructions for this and other listening practices are in the *Teacher's Manual.*

Listening: Look at the factory plan on page 26. Your teacher will tell you where you are and then give you directions like the following to another place.

■ | Go out and | turn right.
| turn left.

| Go downstairs. At the bottom of the stairs, go straight.

| Go upstairs. At the top of the stairs, take a left.

| Go past | the shop.
| the office.

| At the end of the hall, turn right.

| At the first hall, turn left.

FLOOR PLAN OF AHMED'S FACTORY

SECOND FLOOR

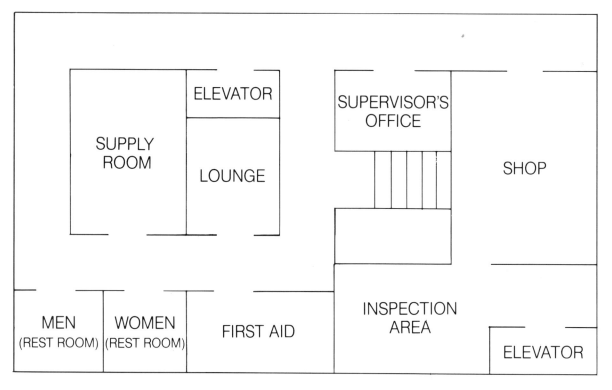

FIRST FLOOR

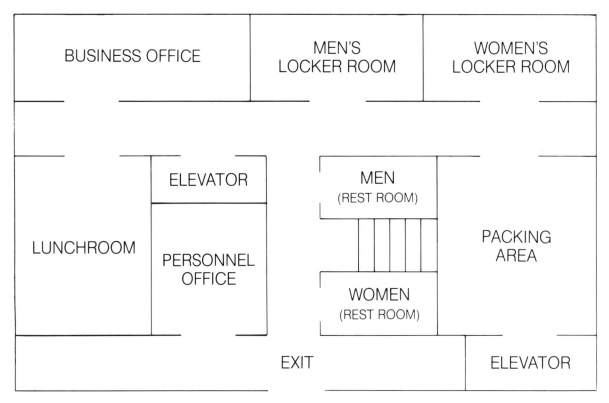

Practice 2

Use the factory plan again and practice asking and giving directions.

Example: You want to go from the shop to the supply room.
■ How do I get to the supply room?
□ Go out and turn left. Take a left at the hall. At the end of the hall, turn right. It's the second door on the right.
■ Thanks.

1. You want to go from the shop to the packing area.
2. You want to go from the lunchroom to the shop.
3. You want to go from the women's locker room to the shop.
4. You want to go from the supply room to the personnel office.
5. Make up your own questions.

5. Asking and telling where supplies are kept

 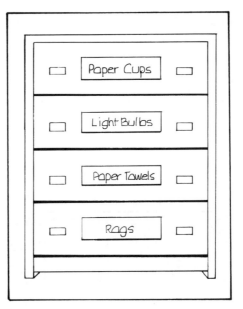

■ Where's the toilet paper?
□ It's on the top shelf.

■ Where's the soap?
□ It's on the bottom shelf.

■ Where are the sponges?
□ They're on the second shelf from the top.

■ I can't find the paper cups.
□ They're in the top drawer.

■ I can't find the rags.
□ They're in the bottom drawer.

■ I can't find the paper towels.
□ They're in the second drawer from the bottom.

■ Where do you keep the toilet bowl cleaner?
□ It's in the top right-hand cabinet.

■ Where did you put the mop?
□ It's in the bottom left-hand cabinet.

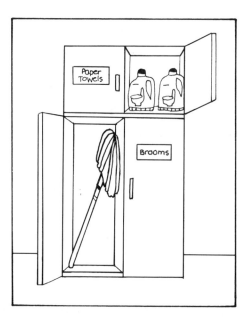

Practice

Listening: Listen to your teacher's directions and write the number in the correct place.

Example: On the top shelf

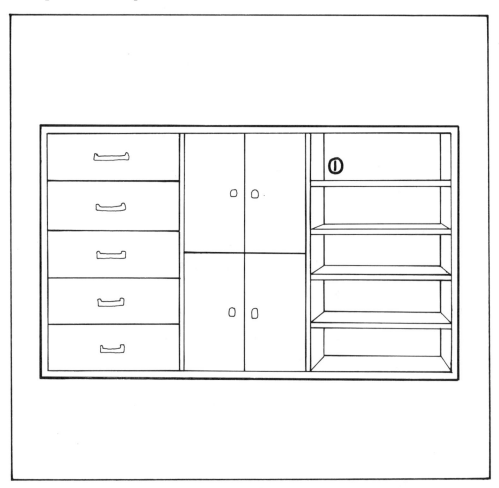

6. Clarifying when you don't understand directions

■ I can't find the rags.

□ They're in the bottom drawer.

■ Where?

□ In the bottom drawer.

■ Okay, thanks.

■ Where do you keep the mop?

□ In the bottom right-hand closet.

■ In the bottom right-hand closet?

□ Right.

■ Thanks.

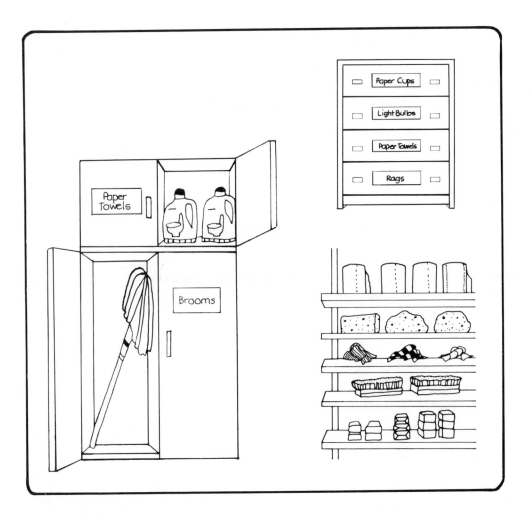

Practice

Look at the picture and practice conversations like those above with your partner.
Ask a different question each time.

1. toilet paper
2. mop
3. paper towels
4. toilet bowl cleaner

5. rags
6. sponges
7. paper cups
8. light bulbs

Role-plays

Student A	Student B
1. You ask a friend where the rest room or some other place is at your school.	Answer your partner.
2. You ask someone you don't know how to get to the office or some other place in your school.	Answer your partner.
3. You can't find the paper or something else at your school. You ask a friend where it's kept.	Answer your partner.

Using What You've Learned

At school or work, practice these two conversations:
1. Ask how to get somewhere and see if you can follow the instructions.
2. Ask where some supplies are stored and then see if you can find them.

Tell your classmates whom you spoke to and what happened.

Training Exercise

Note to the teacher: Complete instructions for leading your students in this training exercise are in the *Teacher's Manual*.

Note to the students: In this exercise you will take part in a factory assembly line. Follow your teacher's instructions carefully.

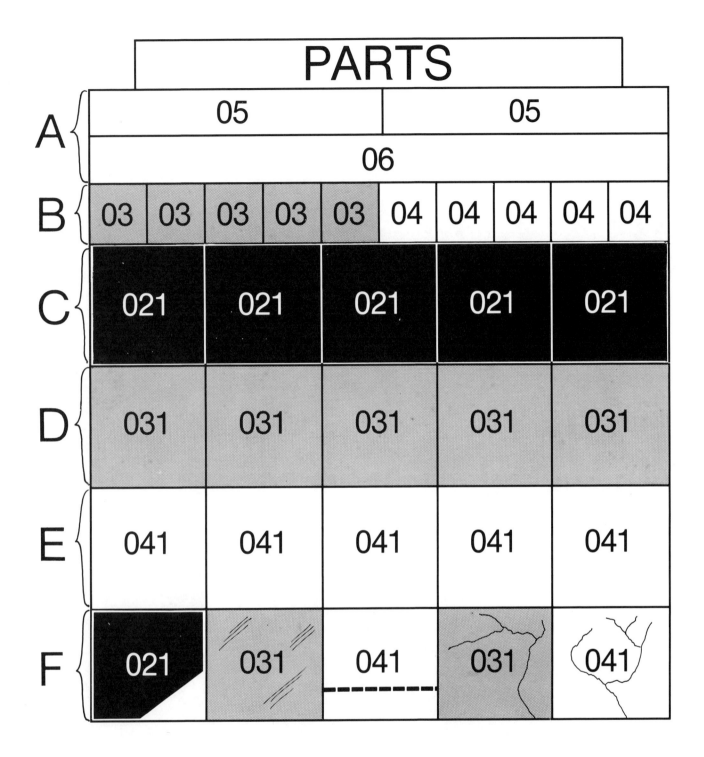

PARTS

| A | 05 | | 05 | |
| B | 03 03 03 03 03 | 04 04 04 04 04 | | |

Understanding Time Clocks and Time Sheets

Time Clocks

Many factories and offices use time clocks to count the hours an employee works. For each pay period, the employee is given a time card on which his hours are recorded.

Arriving at work: When the worker arrives at work, he puts his card in the time clock and the machine prints his starting time on the card. This is called punching in.

33

Leaving work: When the worker finishes work, he puts his card in the time clock again and his finishing time is printed on the card. This is called punching out.

Sometimes a worker forgets to punch in or out. If this happens, the worker should tell his supervisor right away so she can record the worker's starting or finishing time by hand.

When the employer wants to pay a worker, she looks at the time card and knows exactly how many hours the worker has worked. The employer can also see if the worker has worked overtime or if the worker has been arriving at work on time.

Time Sheets

In workplaces where there are no time clocks, employees must fill in time sheets so their employers will know when and how long they have worked. Workers usually hand in time sheets once a week or every two weeks, but it is important for them to fill in their time sheets every day so they won't forget how many hours they have worked.

Practice 1

Study the time sheet below, then answer the questions.

House Cleaners, Inc.

TIME SHEET

__Lin Fong_____   __2/9/85_____
Employee's Name   *Pay Period Ending*

	AM In	Lunch Out	Lunch In	PM Out	Total Daily Hours
Sunday	—	—	—	—	—
Monday	8:00	12:00	1:00	5:00	8
Tuesday	—	—	1:00	5:00	4
Wednesday	8:00	12:00	1:00	5:00	8
Thursday	—	—	1:00	5:00	4
Friday	8:00	12:00	1:00	5:00	8
Saturday	—	—	—	—	—

____*Lin Fong*_____   ___32___
Employee's Signature   *Total Hours*

---

1. Is this time sheet for the week of Feb. 3 to 9 or Feb. 9 to 15? _____

2. When is Lin's lunch break? _____ How long is it? _____

3. What days did Lin start work at 8:00? _____

4. What days did he only work in the afternoon? _____

5. How many hours did he work on Monday? _____

6. What days did he work full-time? _____

7. What were Lin's total hours for the week? _____

8. Who signs the time sheet? _____ Why? _____

Practice 2

Read about Suzanne Wong and then fill in her time sheet.

Suzanne is a teacher at the International Institute. Monday to Friday she taught a class from 12:15 to 2:15 in the afternoon. On Monday and Wednesday mornings, she did office work from 9:00 to 11:00. On Friday morning, she typed lessons and corrected papers from 9:00 to 11:00. Fill in Suzanne's time sheet for the week of February 3 to 9. You can sign Suzanne's name.

TIME SHEET

Employee				Pay Period Ending	
	IN	**OUT**	**IN**	**OUT**	**Total Daily Hours**
Sun.					
Mon.					
Tues.					
Wed.					
Thur.					
Fri.					
Sat.					
Employee's Signature				Total Hours	

Using What You've Learned

If you are working, bring in a time sheet from your workplace and practice filling it in. If you are not working, fill in this time sheet with your school hours for two weeks of this month.

TIME SHEET				
DATE	**IN**	**OUT**	**REASON FOR ABSENCE**	**NUMBER OF HOURS**
			TOTAL HOURS	

3

Talking About Your Family

Conversation

It's 10:00 in the morning. Alicia and Jane are talking during their coffee break. They just met a few days ago.

Alicia: Jane, are you married?

Jane: Yes, I am.

Alicia: Do you have any children?

Jane: Yes, one son and two daughters. How about you, Alicia?

Alicia: I don't have any kids yet. I just got married last year. How old are your children?

Jane: My son's 20 and the girls are 16 and 18.

Alicia: Are they all living at home?

Jane: No, just the girls. My son lives at school.

Alicia: What's he studying?

Jane: He's studying to be a computer programmer.

Alicia: That's great! And your husband. What does he do?

Jane: He's a carpenter. How about yours?

Alicia: He's a mechanic.

Jane: Oh, it's time to go.

Alicia: Yes, it is! See you at lunch.

Write T for true and F for false.

_____ 1. Jane and Alicia met about a year ago.

_____ 2. Jane and Alicia are having lunch.

_____ 3. Jane is married and has three children.

_____ 4. Alicia is single and doesn't have any children.

_____ 5. Jane has one son and two daughters.

_____ 6. Jane's daughters are living at home.

_____ 7. Jane's son is studying to be a carpenter.

_____ 8. Alicia is going to see Jane at lunch.

Useful Expressions

1. Asking if people are married or single

■ Are you married?	□ Yes, I am.
	No, I'm a widow/widower.
	divorced.
	single.

Practice

Practice conversations like this. Talk about yourself.

■ Are you married?

□ Yes, I am. How about you?

■ No, I'm single.

2. Asking people about their children

■ Do you have any Any	children? kids?	□	Yes,	I do. I have one son and two daughters.
			No,	I don't. not yet.

■ How many children do you have? How many?	□	I have two sons. I've got one. I don't have any.

■ How old	are they? is your	son? daughter?	□	They're five and eleven. He's twelve. She is five.

Practice

Practice a conversation like this. Talk about your own family.

■ Do you have any children?
□ Yes, I have one son and two daughters.
■ How old are they?
□ They're six, seven, and ten.

3. Asking about people's occupations

■ What does your husband do?
□ He's a welder. How about yours?
■ He's a mechanic.

■ What does your wife do?
□ She's a housewife. How about yours?
■ She's an assembler.

Practice

Practice conversations like the ones above about your family.

4. Returning a question

- ■ Are you married?
- □ Yes, I am. How about you?
- ■ Yes, I'm married, too.

- ■ Is your husband working?
- □ Yes, he is. How about yours?
- ■ No, he's going to school.

Practice

Ask a question to which a second student responds and returns a question. Use the questions below.

1. Do you have children?
2. How many children do you have?
3. Are you working?
4. What does your husband/wife do?

5. Ending your conversation

- ■ Oh, it's time to go!
- □ I have to go, too. Bye.

- ■ Time to go!
- □ Right! Let's go.

- ■ Break's over.
- □ See you later.

Practice

Practice conversations like this with your partner.

- ■ Time to go!
- □ Right! See you at lunch.

Role-plays

You and a new friend are having coffee together. Ask each other questions about your families. Don't let your partner ask you more than two questions before you return a question. End your conversation when break is over.

In the U.S.

A. What's wrong with these conversations?

1. **Jane:** How many kids do you have?
   Alicia: Two boys.
   Jane: How old are they?
   Alicia: They're five and twelve.
   Jane: How old are you, Alicia?

2. **John:** What does your wife do?
   Paul: She's a computer programmer.
   John: How much does she make?

B. What kinds of things do Americans like to talk about and what things are not acceptable to talk about? Try this true/false quiz and see how much you know.

_____ 1. Americans love to talk about the weather.

_____ 2. It is not okay to ask adults how old they are.

_____ 3. Americans like to talk about their families.

_____ 4. It's okay to ask people why they are divorced.

_____ 5. It's okay to ask people how much their new house cost.

_____ 6. Americans like to talk about sports.

_____ 7. It's all right to ask married people why they don't have children.

_____ 8. It's okay to ask people how much money they make.

_____ 9. It's okay to ask people how their work is going.

_____ 10. It's all right to ask people what religion they are.

Using What You've Learned

At work this week, talk to someone you would like to know better. Find out a little about him and his family. Answer questions about your own family.
Tell your classmates whom you spoke to and what you found out.

Asking for Help

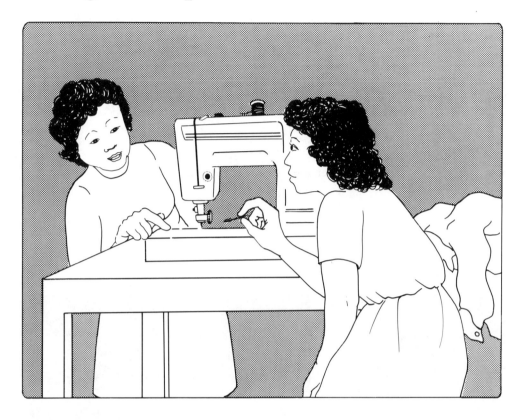

Conversation 1

Rosa is sewing at her machine when the needle breaks.

Rosa: Excuse me, Ann. Can you help me, please?
Ann: Sure. What's the problem?
Rosa: My needle just broke and I don't know how to change it.
Ann: No problem. Let me show you. First unscrew this screw and take out the needle.
Rosa: I see.
Ann: Now put the new needle with the flat side to the right and tighten the screw. Do you understand?
Rosa: I'm not sure. Can you show me again?
Ann: Sure. Put the needle with the flat side to the right and tighten the screw.
Rosa: Okay, I get it now. Thanks a lot.

Write T for true and F for false.

_____ 1. Rosa is sewing by hand.

_____ 2. Rosa's sewing machine is broken.

_____ 3. Rosa can't change the needle.

_____ 4. Rosa doesn't ask Ann for help.

_____ 5. Ann shows Rosa how to change the needle.

_____ 6. Ann is happy to help Rosa.

Useful Expressions

1. Asking someone to help you

| ■ Excuse me. Can you help me, please? | □ Sure. What's the problem? |

| ■ I can't fix
 I don't know how
　　to fix | this machine. | □ Here, let me show you.
 Let me explain it to you. |

Practice 1

Look at each picture below and state the problem.

 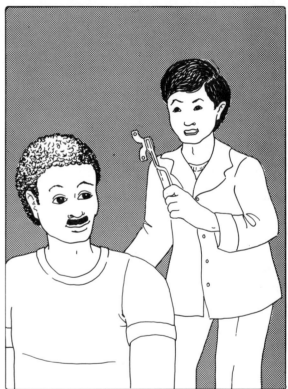

Example: *open this jar*

　　　　I can't *open this jar*.

1. work this can opener

. . . .

44

2. find the typing paper

. . . .

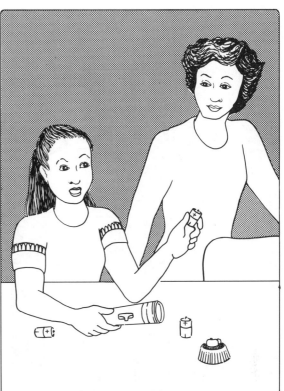

3. change these batteries

. . . .

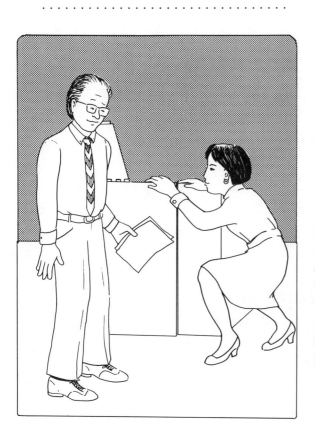

4. fix this machine

. . . .

5. turn off this machine

. . . .

45

6. read this note

7. fill out this form

. . . .

Practice 2

Look at the pictures again. Ask someone to help you and state what your problem is.

■ Could you help me, please?
□ Sure. What's the problem?
■ I can't open this jar.
□ Here. Let me help you.

2. Asking someone to show you something

■ I can't change this needle.
□ Let me show you. (Helper demonstrates.)
■ I still don't understand. Can you show me again?

3. Asking someone to watch you

■ I can't thread this machine.
□ Let me show you. (Helper demonstrates.)
■ Okay. Can you watch me do it?

Practice

Your teacher or another student will show you how to change the batteries in a tape recorder or how to put staples in a stapler or some other task. After watching this, ask your helper to show you again or to watch you do it.

Conversation 2

Rosa is having trouble filling out a form for her job. She is asking her lead worker for help.

Rosa: Ann, can you help me a minute? I've run out of thread and I'm not sure how to fill out this supply form.
Ann: Let me see. You write your employee number here.
Rosa: Okay. And what do I write here?
Ann: The color number for the thread.
Rosa: Color number 024. And what does this mean?
Ann: Q-N-T-Y means quantity. You put how many you need.
Rosa: I see. And do I sign here?
Ann: Right. And put the date.
Rosa: Okay. I get it. Thanks, Ann.

Answer these questions:

1. What has Rosa run out of?
2. Why does she ask Ann for help?
3. Did Rosa understand QNTY? What does it mean?
4. What three questions does Rosa ask to get the form filled out?

_____

_____

_____

# 12349			
■■■ **SUPPLY REQUEST** ■■■			
Qnty.	Item	Size	Color
1	thread	L	024

6/14/85
Date

Rosa Rodriguez
Signature

Useful Expressions

1. Useful questions for filling out forms

A. If you don't understand or can't read something written

■ | What does this | word | mean?
      | | number |
   | What does this mean?

B. If you don't know what to write on a certain line

■ | What do I | write | here?
      | | put |

C. If you think you have to sign, but you're not sure

■ | Where do I sign?
   | Do I sign here?

D. If you don't know how to spell a word

■ How do you spell _____ ?

2. Telling someone that you have run out of something

■ | I've run out of | thread.
   | I need some more |

Practice

Practice a conversation like this with your partner. Substitute a different word each time.

Example: *paper*
■ Can you help me, please?
□ Sure. What's the problem?
■ I've run out of *paper*.

1. thread
2. zippers
3. needles
4. buttons

Training Exercise

Note to the teacher: Complete instructions for leading this training exercise appear in the *Teacher's Manual*.

Note to the student: Your teacher will give you a list of supplies you need. Fill out this supply form, and don't forget to ask for help if there is anything you don't understand.

# _____		Dept. _____		
		SUPPLY REQUEST		
Amount	**Item Name**	**Part #**	**Color**	**Size**

_____
Signature

_____
Date

_____
Signature

In the U.S.

Read this problem. Then circle what you think is the best answer.

Stan has to clean floors where he works. He knows what detergent to use, but he doesn't know how much to use. What should he do?

a. Clean without detergent since he doesn't know how much to use.

b. Guess how much detergent to use.

c. Ask his supervisor or another worker how much detergent to use.

Understanding Paychecks

Paychecks

In this unit, you will learn how to read and understand your paycheck. You will also learn to check your paycheck for mistakes.

Paychecks and pay stubs: This is a paycheck and a pay stub. Before you cash your check, you should always check your pay stub to make sure that your pay is correct.

MERRILL, INC.   No. 5283

April 26, 1985

Pay to the
Order of

Ann Johnson $ 391.77

Three Hundred Ninety-one and 77/100

Virginia Merrill

1:9003891:317001:220:9

- -

NAME: ANN JOHNSON

Regular Hours	Overtime Hours	Regular Pay	Overtime Pay	Gross Pay	Period Ending
80	15	400.00	112.50	512.50	4/27/85

Deductions This Pay Period

Fed. With. Tax	F.I.C.A.	State Tax	Insurance	Union Dues
45.92	33.50	28.81	12.50	00.00

Gross Pay	Net Pay	Gross Pay	Fed. Tax.	F.I.C.A.	State Tax	Insurance	Union Dues
512.50	391.77	2850.00	202.92	187.60	124.79	50.00	00.00

Earnings This Pay Period	**Year-To-Date Totals**

Pay periods: What is the date under *period ending* on this pay stub? _____. This date means that this check is for the two weeks before April 27, 1985. April 27 is the last day you are being paid for by this check. You are being paid for the circled days.

APRIL • 1985						
Su	M	T	W	Th	F	Sa
	1	2	3	4	5	6
7	8	9	10	11	12	13
(14)	(15)	(16)	(17)	(18)	(19)	(20)
(21)	(22)	(23)	(24)	(25)	(26)	(27)
28	29	30				

Pay periods are not the same at all workplaces. Sometimes workers are paid on the 15th and on the 30th/31st of each month. At some workplaces, workers are paid every other week on the same day, and at others workers are paid every week. Each worker must find out what the pay period is at his workplace.

Study this pay stub and the definitions on the next page. Each numbered arrow points to where that defined term appears on the pay stub.

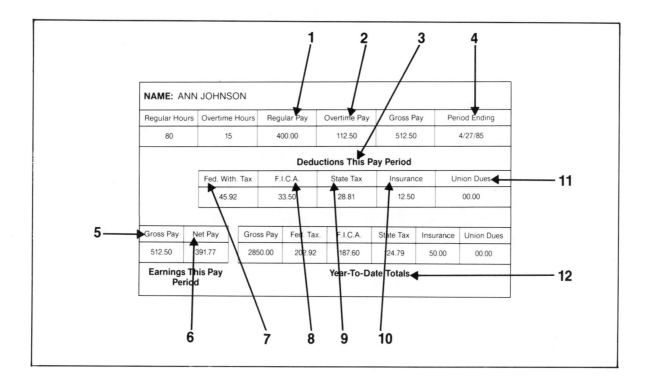

51

Definitions

1. <u>Regular Pay</u>: Pay for hours that are not overtime.
2. <u>Overtime Pay</u>: Pay for extra hours worked.
3. <u>Deductions</u>: Money subtracted from your earnings.
4. <u>Pay Period Ending/Period Ending</u>: The last day you are being paid for with this check.
5. <u>Gross Pay/Total Earnings</u>: Total pay before deductions.
6. <u>Net Pay/Take-home Pay</u>: Total pay after deductions.
7. <u>Federal Withholding Tax</u>: Tax taken out of your check by the U.S. government.
8. <u>F.I.C.A.</u>: Social Security.
9. <u>State Withholding Tax</u>: Tax taken out by the state.
10. <u>Health Insurance</u>: Money paid to your insurance plan.
11. <u>Union Dues</u>: Money paid to your union.
12. <u>Year-to-date Totals</u>: How much tax and other deductions you have paid so far this year.

Practice 1

Match the term in column B with the appropriate term in column A.

A	B
_____ 1. gross pay	a. take-home pay
_____ 2. F.I.C.A.	b. Social Security
_____ 3. net pay	c. state withholding tax
_____ 4. fed. with. tax	d. total earnings
_____ 5. state with. tax	e. federal withholding tax

Practice 2

Look at the following pay stubs and answer the questions.

NAME: CATHY WATSON					
Regular Hours	Overtime Hours	Regular Pay	Overtime Pay	Gross Pay	Period Ending
80		486.00		486.00	3/29/85

Deductions This Pay Period					
	Fed. With. Tax	F.I.C.A.	State Tax	Insurance	Union Dues
	50.71	32.56	26.04	00.00	00.00

Gross Pay	Net Pay		Gross Pay	Fed. Tax.	F.I.C.A.	State Tax	Insurance	Union Dues
486.00	376.69		2,943.00	309.28	197.17	153.13	00.00	00.00
Earnings This Pay Period			**Year-To-Date Totals**					

1. What is the last day of the pay period for this check? _____

   _____

2. Did Cathy work overtime this pay period? _____

3. How much was deducted for Social Security this month? _____

   _____

4. How much federal tax did she pay this month? _____

5. What was her take-home pay this pay period? _____

6. Does Cathy have health insurance deducted from her check? _____

   _____

Pay Period End			Employee Number	Dept.	Hours Worked	Overtime Hours	Base Pay	Overtime Pay
Mo	Day	Yr	3824	6	80 | 0	6 | 0	360 | 00	40 | 50
02	28	85						

	Gross Earnings	Federal Withhold. Tax	State Tax	F.I.C.A.	Insur.	Union Dues	Net Pay
Week	400 | 50	31 | 50	19 | 84	26 | 80	0 | 0	12 | 00	310 | 36
Year	1300 | 00	88 | 00	53 | 62	87 | 10	0 | 0	24 | 00	1047 | 28

KEEP THIS STUB
It is a record
of your earnings.

SIDNEY'S A-1 SERVICE

1. How many regular hours did this person work? _____

2. What was his regular pay? _____

3. What was his overtime pay? _____

4. What was his gross pay? _____

5. How much did he pay in federal and state taxes? _____

6. How much was deducted for insurance? _____

7. What was his take-home pay this paycheck? _____

8. What was the last day of the pay period? _____

9. How much has he paid in Social Security this year? _____

_____

10. How much has he earned so far this year before taxes? _____

_____

Practice 3

Finding mistakes on your paycheck: Study the formulas below and then do the problems.

regular pay   =   regular hours   ×   regular hourly pay

overtime pay   =   overtime hours ×   overtime hourly pay

gross pay   =   regular pay   +   overtime pay

take-home pay =   gross pay   −   deductions

A. Jim worked 35 hours this week. He is paid $7.50 an hour.
The following deductions were made on his check:

federal tax $23.50
state tax $15.00
F.I.C.A. $11.00

1. What was Jim's gross pay? _____

2. What were his total deductions? _____

3. What was his take-home pay? _____

B. Kay worked 40 hours this week at $9 an hour. She worked 8 hours overtime
at $13.50 an hour. The following deductions were made on her check:

federal tax $46.50
state tax $28.16
F.I.C.A. $21.20
insurance $12.00

1. What is Kay's regular pay? _____

2. What is Kay's overtime pay? _____

3. What is Kay's gross pay? _____

4. What are Kay's total deductions? _____

5. What is Kay's take-home pay? _____

Using What You've Learned

Look at one of your own pay stubs and answer as many of the following
questions as you can. If you are not working, ask a family member or friend for
a pay stub. If you don't have one, your teacher will give you one to work with.

1. What pay period is this check for? _____

2. Did you work overtime during this pay period? _____

3. Does your pay stub tell you how many hours you worked? _____

_____

4. What was your gross pay for this pay period? _____

5. How much was deducted for Social Security for this pay period? _____

_____

6. How much was deducted for federal and state taxes? _____

_____

7. List other deductions on your pay stub.

_____ $ _____

_____ $ _____

_____ $ _____

8. How much was your take-home pay? _____

9. How much money have you made so far this year before taxes? _____

_____

10. How much federal and state tax have you paid so far this year? _____

_____

In the U.S.

Alberto started work on July 1. He worked one week, and on July 5 he filled out his time sheet for the week he worked. One week later, on July 12, Alberto and the other workers were paid. Alberto was very upset because he had worked two weeks and was paid for only one. Can you explain why Alberto was paid for just one week? If not, the following questions will help you:

1. How many weeks did Alberto work?
2. How many weeks did he write on his time sheet?
3. How many weeks was he paid for?
4. When will he fill in his next time sheet?
5. How many weeks will he write on that one?
6. How many weeks will he be paid for?

JULY • 1985						
Su	M	T	W	Th	F	Sa
	1	2	3	4	⑤	6
7	8	9	10	11	🔲12	13
14	15	16	17	18	⑲	20
21	22	23	24	25	🔲26	27
28	29	30	31			

○ time sheet day
☐ pay day

Talking About Your Job

Conversation 1

Karl is talking to a friend at a bus stop while waiting to get his bus.

Jan: Hi, Karl.
Karl: Hi, Jan. How's it going?
Jan: Not bad. Say, are you working yet?
Karl: I sure am.
Jan: That's great. Where?
Karl: At Bright Building Maintenance.
Jan: What kind of work do you do?
Karl: I'm a janitor.
Jan: How do you like the work?
Karl: It's not bad.

Jan: This is my bus. See you tomorrow.
Karl: Bye, Jan.

Write T for true and F for false.

_____ 1. Karl has a job now.

_____ 2. Karl's a janitor.

_____ 3. Karl doesn't like his job.

Conversation 2

Karl is talking to a new friend during break.

Al: Hi, Karl.
Karl: Hi. I'm sorry. I forgot your name.
Al: Al, Al Johnson.
Karl: Al Johnson?
Al: Right.
Karl: Al, what do you do here?
Al: I'm a machine operator. I clean and wax floors. How about you?
Karl: I'm a general cleaner. I clean offices.
Al: How long have you been with B. B. M.?
Karl: Just two weeks.
Al: How do you like it?
Karl: Fine. The work's not too bad.
Al: Good. Well, see you around, Karl.
Karl: Bye, Al.

Write T for true and F for false.

_____ 1. Karl can't remember Al's name.

_____ 2. Al is a general cleaner.

_____ 3. Karl's been working at B.B.M. for two months.

_____ 4. Karl likes his job.

Useful Expressions

1. Talking about whether you're working

■ Are you	working	now?	□	Yes, I am.
	employed			I sure am.
				No, I got laid off.

■ Do you have a job yet? □ I sure do.
No, | not yet.
| I'm still looking.

2. Talking about where people work

■ Where | do you work? □ At | St. John's Hospital.
| are you working? | a hospital.
| Denny's Restaurant.
| a restaurant.

3. Talking about the kind of work you do

■ What | do you do? □ | I'm a janitor.
| kind of work do you do? | I clean offices.

Practice

Practice conversations like the following with your partner. Substitute a different answer each time.

Example: *St. John's Hospital/nurse*
■ Are you working now?
□ I sure am.
■ Where?
□ At *St. John's Hospital.*
■ What kind of work do you do?
□ I'm a *nurse.*

1. a hospital/work in the laundry
2. not working
3. a restaurant/bus boy
4. a school/janitor
5. the Brown Shoe Company/sell shoes
6. a shoe factory/make boots

4. Talking about how long you've worked

■ How long | worked here? □ | I just started.
have you | been working here? | About 4 months.
| worked at St. John's? | For two years.
| Since 1979.

5. Talking about how you like your work

■ How do you like	the work?	□	It's okay.
	your job?		It's not bad.
	working here?		I like it.
	it here?		

Practice

Practice conversations like the following with your partner. Substitute a different answer each time.

Example: *janitor/a week*

■ What do you do here?
□ I'm a *janitor*.
■ How long have you been working here?
□ About *a week*.
■ How do you like the work?
□ It's not bad.

1. machine operator/a month
2. kitchen helper/two weeks

3. mail clerk/since June
4. cook/one year

6. Finding out a name you've forgotten

■ Hi, Jenise.
□ Hi. I'm sorry. I forgot your name.
■ Ann, Ann Robins.
□ Ann Robins?
■ Right.

Practice

Practice the conversation above with your partner. Use your own names.

Role-plays

Student A

1. You see a friend and ask him if he's working now. You ask him what he does. You ask him how long he's been working and if he likes his job.

2. You say *Hi* to a worker you met yesterday. You ask her what she does. You ask her if she likes her job.

Student B

You are working at a school. You're a janitor. You clean classrooms and you have worked there for a month. You like your job.

You can't remember the worker's name. You're a mail worker. You sort mail. You like your job.

3. You see a friend. You ask him if he's working. You are working at the First National Bank. You are a teller. You like your job.

   You got laid off. You ask a friend if she's working. You ask where she's working and what her job is. You ask if she likes her job.

4. You say *Hi* to a friend you met last week. You are working as a seamstress. You are working at home. You like working at home because you can be with your children.

   You see someone you met last week, but you can't remember her name. You ask if she's working and what her job is. You ask her where she works. You ask her how she likes her job.

Showing Concern for Safety

Conversation 1

Kim just started work yesterday. The foreman comes by before Kim starts his morning work.

Kim: Morning.
John: Morning. You're new here, right?
Kim: Yes, I just started work yesterday. My name's Kim Nguyen.
John: Nice to meet you, Kim. I'm John Parker, your foreman.
Kim: Happy to meet you, Mr. Parker.
John: Call me John. Any questions about using the grinder?
Kim: No, thanks. I know how to work it now.
John: Okay. Don't forget your safety glasses.
Kim: No, I won't. Thanks, John.

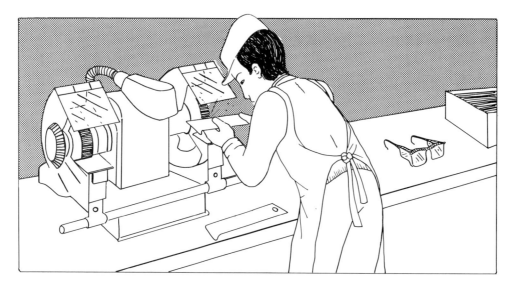

Conversation 2

About an hour later, Kim's foreman sees him working without his safety glasses.

John: Kim, you should wear your safety glasses. You could hurt your eyes.
Kim: You're right. I should be more careful.
John: Besides, wearing safety glasses is a company rule.
Kim: It is?
John: Yes. You could lose your job if you don't use them.
Kim: Thanks for telling me, John.
John: That's okay.

Write T for true and F for false.

_____ 1. Kim has been working at the factory for two weeks.

_____ 2. He's a saw operator.

_____ 3. He's not sure how to run his machine.

_____ 4. Kim has to wear safety glasses for his work.

_____ 5. Kim forgot to wear his safety glasses.

_____ 6 The safety glasses protect his eyes.

_____ 7. Wearing safety glasses isn't a company rule.

_____ 8. Kim could lose his job if he doesn't wear his safety glasses.

Useful Expressions

1. Introducing yourself to a co-worker

■ You're new here, right?
□ Yes, I just started yesterday. My name's Kim Nguyen.
■ Nice to meet you, Kim. I'm John Parker.
□ Nice to meet you, John.

2. Getting someone to repeat his name

- ■ My name's Kim Nguyen.
- □ I'm sorry. What's your name again?
- ■ Kim Nguyen.
- □ Nice to meet you, Kim.

Practice

Practice conversations like the ones above with a partner.

3. Reminding people to use safety equipment

- ■ Don't forget (to use) your safety glasses.
- □ I won't. Thanks for reminding me.

- ■ Remember (to wear) your ear plugs.
- □ I will. Thanks for reminding me.

Practice 1

1. Tell your teacher the names of the equipment you know and then ask about the ones that are new to you.
2. Listen to your teacher and point to the equipment he/she names. Then name the equipment yourself.
3. Match the pictures and the words. Write the letter of the picture in front of the correct word.

_____ goggles

_____ ear muffs

_____ hard hat

_____ ear plugs

_____ gloves

_____ apron

_____ face shield

_____ safety glasses

_____ work shoes

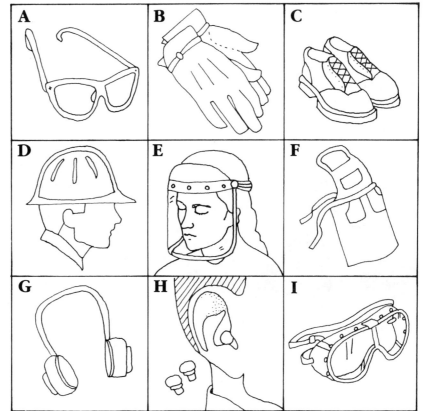

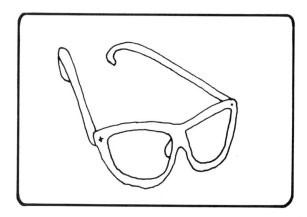

Practice 2

Look at the pictures again and practice conversations like these:

- Don't forget to use your safety glasses.
- □ I won't. Thanks for reminding me.

- Remember to use your safety glasses.
- □ I will.

4. Talking about dangerous situations

- The scissors could fall on his foot.
  Her hair could get caught in the machine.
  He could lose his hearing.
  He could get something in his eyes.
  She could hurt her head.
  She could │ hurt her skin.
           │ get a rash.

Practice

A. Your teacher will describe a dangerous situation. Point to the picture he/she describes.

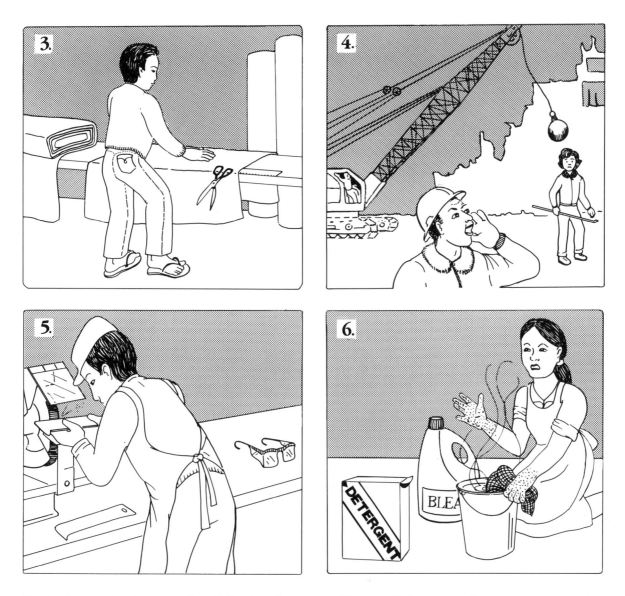

B. Look at each picture again. Tell what dangerous thing could happen and what the worker should do.

- ■ What could happen?
- ☐ Her hair could get caught in the machine.
- ■ What should she do?
- ☐ She should tie back her hair.

5. Understanding company rules

- ■ Wearing ear plugs is a company rule.
- ☐ Gee, thanks for telling me. I didn't know.

- ■ You're required to tie back your hair.
- ☐ That's good to know. Thanks for telling me.

Practice

Look at the pictures of dangerous situations again and practice conversations like the ones on the preceding page about company rules.

6. Warning people

■ | Look out!
Look out! The machine guard is up!
Look out for | the cord!
| your fingers!

■ | Watch out!
Watch out for | the crane!
| your head!
Watch out! The floor's slippery.

■ | Don't touch that!
Don't touch that! The wire's frayed.
Don't touch that plug! Your feet are wet.

■ | Stop!
Be careful!
Don't move!

Practice

A. Listen to your teacher's warning and point to the correct picture below.

B. Practice warning the person you see in the picture. Write the warning beneath each picture.

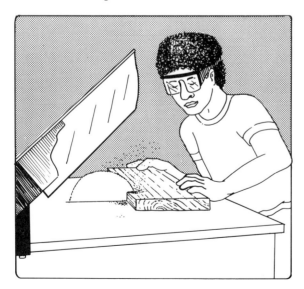 

Example:

Look out! The machine guard is up.   1. . . . .

2. . . . .

3. . . . .

4. . . . .

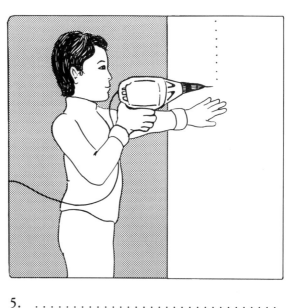

5. . . . .

Role-plays

Supervisor

1. You see a worker you don't know. You ask her if she's new. You remind her to wear her goggles.

2. You see a worker without his hard hat. You have seen him without his hat before. You tell him he must wear a hat; it's a company rule.

Worker

You are new at this job. You started last week. You are happy that your supervisor reminded you about your goggles.

You didn't know that wearing a hat was a company rule. Thank your supervisor for telling you.

Training Exercise

Note to the teacher: Complete instructions for leading your students in this training exercise are in the *Teacher's Manual*.

Note to the students: In this exercise you will review Unit 1, Section 2, in which you learned what to do when you don't understand instructions. For this exercise you will use your envelope of parts and this board.

BOARD   # _____

	A	**B**	**C**	**D**
1				
2				
3				
4				
5				

Understanding Safety Rules

Protective Equipment

Many accidents happen because people don't use protective clothes and equipment. Read about why different kinds of equipment are necessary.

1. Machine operators need goggles, safety glasses, or face masks to keep flying particles and dust out of their eyes. Chemical workers need masks to protect their eyes from splashes.

2. Ear plugs or ear muffs protect the hearing of machine operators and other workers in noisy factories. People can become deaf if their ears are not protected.

3. Gloves and aprons protect workers when they use dangerous chemicals. Workers can get skin rashes if their skin is not protected.

4. Hard hats are used when there is danger from falling or flying objects.

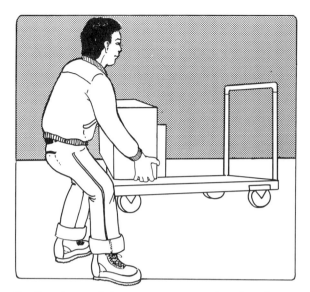 

5. Sturdy workshoes protect people's feet from falling objects. Waterproof boots protect feet from chemicals.

6. Respiratory equipment is used when there are harmful dusts, fumes, or gases in the air. For example, coal miners wear respiratory equipment because there is so much dust in the mines.

Practice

Read about each of the following workers. Then write in what equipment is needed for their jobs.

1. Alice is a saw operator. Woodchips fly in her face and her workplace is very noisy.

   _____

2. Paul runs a grinder. The air is full of flying particles and dust. _____

   _____

3. Kay works in a chemical factory. Chemicals can easily splash on her and there

   are fumes in the air. _____

4. John is a construction worker. Large cranes lower materials to him. _____

   _____

5. Kia is a packer. He lifts and carries things all day. _____

   _____

Safety Rules

Study this list of general safety rules and discuss what kinds of accidents can happen if the rules are not followed.

1. Obey all safety rules and signs.
2. Keep work areas neat and clean.
3. Store tools and equipment safely. Sharp tools should always be stored with points down, for example.

4. Know where fire extinguishers and fire alarms are, and know how to use them.

5. Know where emergency exits are.

6. Know proper use of machines and equipment.

7. Wear protective equipment.

8. Never use equipment with frayed cords. Never overload outlets.

9. Never leave a running machine unattended.

10. Learn the proper way to lift things. Get help to lift heavy loads.

11. Pay attention to warning bells.

12. Know how to get first aid.

13. Report unsafe conditions to your supervisor.

Practice 1

Look at each picture and decide which safety rule is not being followed. Write the rule number from the above list.

Example: ..1.....................   1. ....

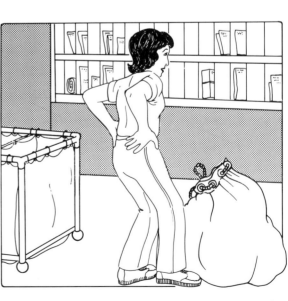

2. ....   3. ....

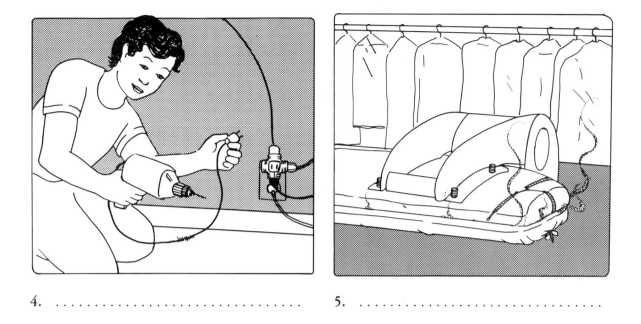

4. . . . . 5. . . . .

Practice 2

Warning signs and safety instructions: Discuss with your class what each of these signs means.

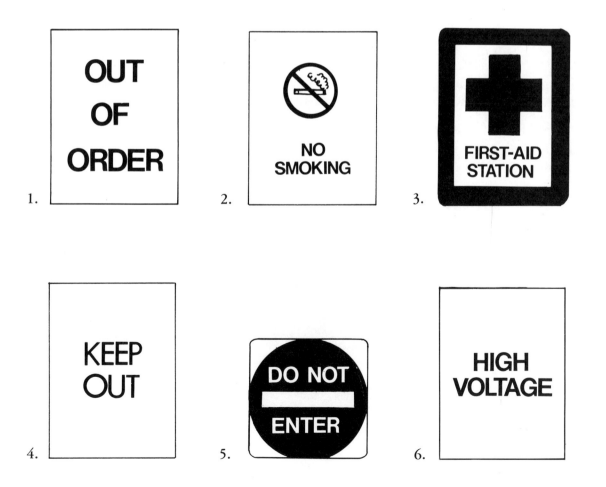

7. USE ONLY WITH GOGGLES

8. SLIPPERY WHEN WET

9. Flammable

10. POISON

11. AUTHORIZED PERSONNEL ONLY

12. DANGER

Using What You've Learned

A. If you are working, bring in a safety manual or safety rules from your work-place. Practice reading them with your classmates.

B. Are there any signs or instructions in your workplace, apartment building, or school that you don't understand? If so, copy them and ask your teacher or classmates about them.

Being Polite

Conversation 1

Marta: I love your hair.
  Did you get it cut?
Susan: Yes. And I had a perm too.
Marta: It looks great.
Susan: Thanks.

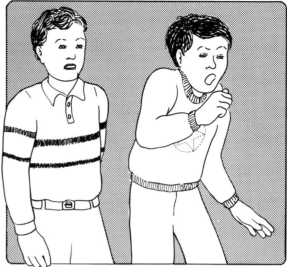

Conversation 2

Solomon: I like that jacket.
Andy: Thanks. I just got it.
Solomon: It looks warm.
Andy: It is.

Conversation 3

Boris: (coughing) Excuse me.
Lou: You really have a bad cough.
Boris: I sure do.

Conversation 4

Thomas: I changed your tire.
Jim: Thanks a lot.
Thomas: You're welcome.

Answer these questions:

1. In the United States, is it okay to tell people that you like their clothes or their hair?
2. What do you say when people say that they like something you have?
3. What should you say when you cough in front of people in the U.S.?
4. What do you say when people help you or do things for you?

76

Useful Expressions

1. Giving and receiving compliments

■ I like your dress.
□ Thanks.

■ Your hair looks great.
□ Thanks a lot.

2. Saying *thank you*

■ Thanks for fixing my car.	□ You're welcome. / No problem.

■ Thank you for this beautiful sweater.	□ You're welcome. / I'm glad you like it.

3. Saying *Excuse me* or *Pardon me*

A. When you cough, burp, or sneeze

Example:
(Someone coughs or burps.)
■ Excuse me.

(Someone sneezes.)
■ Excuse me.
□ God bless you.
■ Thanks.

B. When you have to interrupt people

Example: ■ Excuse me. I have to answer the phone.
        □ No problem.

C. When you want to get someone's attention

Example: ■ Excuse me. Can I see you a minute?
        □ Sure.

D. When you are trying to get by people in a crowd

Example: ■ Excuse me.
        □ (Responds by moving.)

E. When you bump someone

Example: ■ Excuse me.
        □ That's okay.

Practice

Practice a short conversation for each picture and then write your conversation.
Follow the example.

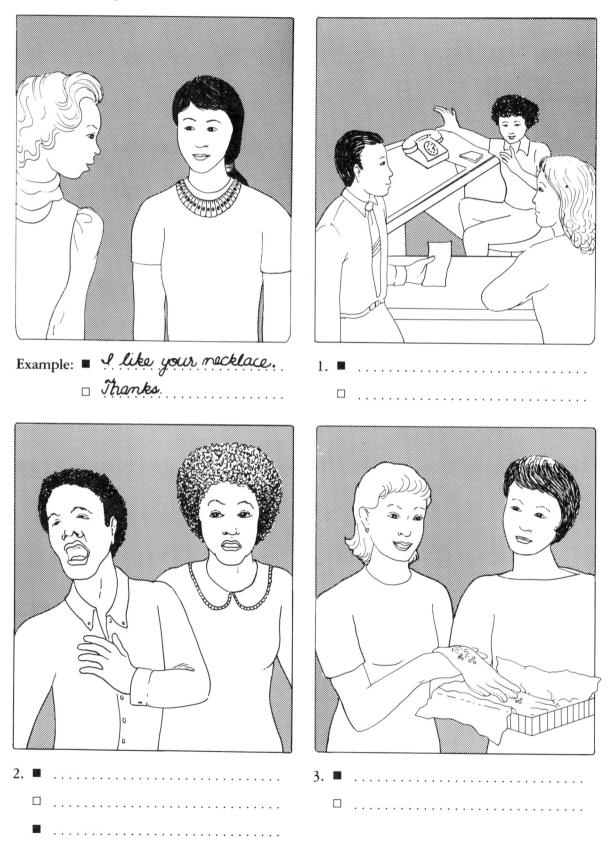

Example: ■ *I like your necklace.*
       □ *Thanks.*

1. ■ . . . .
    □ . . . .

2. ■ . . . .
    □ . . . .
    ■ . . . .

3. ■ . . . .
    □ . . . .

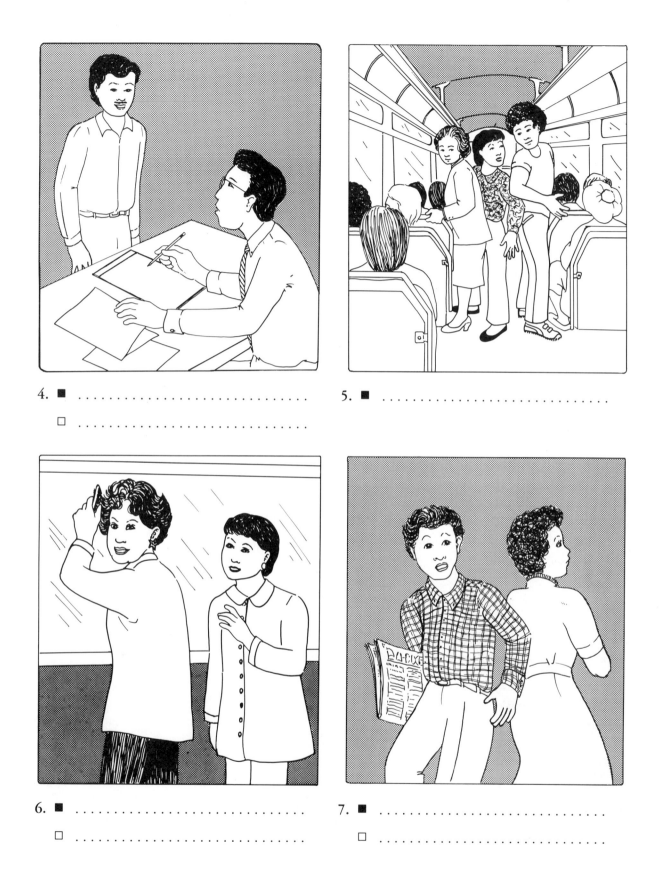

4. ■ . . . .

   □ . . . .

5. ■ . . . .

6. ■ . . . .

   □ . . . .

7. ■ . . . .

   □ . . . .

Conversation 5

Ruth and Helen work together in a restaurant waiting on tables. The restaurant is very busy today.

Ruth: Helen, are you very busy?

Helen: Not really.

Ruth: Listen. Jean's going to be late, and I've got to wait on her tables. Would you mind taking two more tables until she comes?

Helen: Sure. No problem.

Ruth: Thanks a lot. I really appreciate it.

Answer these questions:

1. Why does Ruth have so much work?
2. Is Helen busy too?
3. Why is Ruth very polite when she asks Helen to help her?

Useful Expressions

Making special requests

When you ask co-workers to help with work that they don't usually have to do, you should explain why you need help and also use very polite language.

■ I'm really behind schedule. Would you | help / mind helping | me with this?

□ Sure. No problem.

Practice

In this practice, you will be asking a busy co-worker to do something he doesn't usually do. Choose from the above explanations and polite requests.

Example: *wash these windows*
■ Are you very busy?
□ Not really.
■ I need to finish this by 5:00. Would you help me *wash these windows?*
□ Sure. No problem.
■ Thanks. I really appreciate it.

1. set these tables
2. put away these dishes
3. sweep the floor

Conversation 6

Mrs. Johnson is Nadia's supervisor. She's telling Nadia what work she has to do this morning. Mrs. Johnson is not in a good mood.

Mrs. Johnson: I want you to clean the bathrooms and change all the beds on this floor.
Nadia: I'm sorry, I don't understand. Could you please explain?
Mrs. Johnson: Listen, Nadia. I don't have time to repeat everything for you ten times. I have my own work to do.
Nadia: I know you're busy, Mrs. Johnson, but I don't understand what you want me to do.
Mrs. Johnson: Okay. I want the beds changed and the bathrooms cleaned.
Nadia: Just on this floor, right?
Mrs. Johnson: Right.
Nadia: Thanks, Mrs. Johnson. I know what to do now.

Answer these questions:

1. Who is Mrs. Johnson?
2. Is Mrs. Johnson in a good mood?
3. Does Nadia understand the first time Mrs. Johnson tells her what to do?
4. When Nadia asks her supervisor to repeat, is she rude to Nadia?
5. Does Mrs. Johnson finally repeat the instructions?

Useful Expressions

Responding to rudeness or impatience

■ Please repeat that.
□ I can't repeat everything ten times. I've got my own work to do.
■ I know you're busy, but I don't understand what you want me to do.

■ I'm sorry. I don't understand. Can you please show me again?
□ Hey, I don't have all day to teach you your job.
■ I can see you're busy, but I need to understand what to do or I can't do my job.

Practice

Practice the above conversations with a partner. Then with the help of your teacher, write down other rude comments you have heard or might hear and the responses you could make.

■ _____

□ _____

■ _____

□ _____

Role-plays

Student A	Student B
1. Tell someone in your class that you like something he is wearing or that you like the way his hair looks.	Respond politely.
2. You ask another worker if she can help you mop the kitchen floor. You have to finish by 5:00 so you won't be late for an appointment at the doctor's.	Your friend has helped you with your work before, and you are happy to help her.
3. You are a supervisor. You tell a worker that he is leaving too much cleanser on the sinks when he cleans them. When the worker does not understand, you tell him rudely that you are tired of repeating things for him all the time.	Your supervisor explains something to you, but you don't understand. You ask your supervisor to repeat what she said. Ask your supervisor to repeat, even if she's rude.

Getting Incorrect Work Explained

Conversation 1

Tony is learning to assemble radios. His supervisor comes by to check on his work.

Supervisor: Tony, this is wrong.
Tony: It is? What's wrong with it?
Supervisor: The red wire should connect A2 and B4, not B2.
Tony: Oh, I see. Like this?
Supervisor: That's good, but you'll have to redo this one. Can you see what's wrong?
Tony: No. What's the problem?
Supervisor: Are these transistors the same?
Tony: No, they're not. The A2 transistor is the wrong size.
Supervisor: Right. Now finish it.

Conversation 2

Later Tony finishes his work and checks with his supervisor.

Tony: Ms. Jones, I've finished this. Could you check it for me?
Ms. Jones: Sure. Let's see. This looks good, but C4 will be rejected.
Tony: It will? Why?
Ms. Jones: You didn't attach it correctly. It's too loose.
Tony: You're right. (Tony attaches it again.) Like this?
Ms. Jones: That's good.
Tony: Thanks.

Write T for true and F for false.

_____ 1. Tony is learning to assemble radios.

_____ 2. Tony's supervisor points out mistakes to Tony.

_____ 3. Tony has to redo some of his work.

_____ 4. The supervisor doesn't like to explain things to Tony.

_____ 5. Tony asks his supervisor to check his work.

_____ 6. Tony never thanks his supervisor for help.

Useful Expressions

1. Getting incorrect work explained

■ This isn't right.	□ Can you explain what's wrong with it?
■ This is wrong.	□ It is? What's the problem?
■ You've made a mistake.	□ What is it?
■ These aren't correct. This will be rejected. You'll have to redo this.	□ What's wrong with them? Why? Why? What's the problem?

Practice

Practice conversations like the following with your partner. Use different expressions from above each time.

■ This is wrong.
□ What's wrong with it?

2. Getting your work checked

■ You'll have to redo A4. It's too loose.
□ Like this?
■ Right.

■ Can you check this for me?
□ Sure. That's good.
■ Thanks.

Practice

Practice each of the above conversations with a partner.

3. Pointing out mistakes

■ Are these squares the same?
□ No. This one's the wrong size.

■ Is this square correct?
□ No, it's the wrong color.

4. Describing mistakes

| It's the wrong size. It should be the | large | one.
| | short |

It's the wrong color. It should be black.
It's in the wrong place. It should be | at C4.
| in the top right-hand corner.
| centered.

The connection is wrong. B4 and E7 should be connected.

Practice

Look at the pictures and practice conversations like the example.

Incorrect	**Correct**

Example:
■ Is this correct?   □ It's the wrong size. It should be the small one.

Incorrect	**Correct**

1.

2.

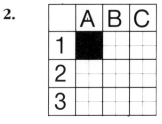 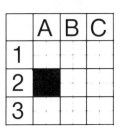

Incorrect   **Correct**

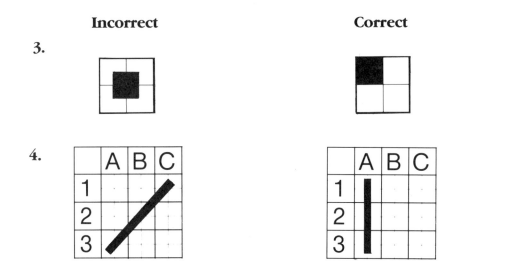

3.

4.

Training Exercise

Note to the teacher: Complete instructions for leading your students in this training exercise are in the *Teacher's Manual*.

Note to the students: In this exercise, you will practice getting mistakes explained and pointing out your own mistakes. You will need the board from page 69 and your envelope of parts. Now listen carefully to your teacher's instructions.

Sample A   **Sample B**

(FOLD HERE)

In the U.S.

Read about the following situations and discuss them with your teacher.

1. Steve works with Tony assembling radios. Steve's supervisor is also Ms. Jones. Steve is usually polite, but sometimes when Ms. Jones corrects him, he is rude to her. Why do you think Steve is not polite to his supervisor, Ms. Jones?

2. Ana makes boots at a shoe factory. She works slowly and carefully, and the boots she makes are always well made. Although she is a hard worker, she is often behind schedule. Her supervisor is worried that he may have to lay her off. What is the problem?

Fire Prevention

Safety Precautions

The following safety precautions can help prevent fire in your home.

1. Don't smoke in bed.
2. Don't overload outlets.
3. Don't use frayed electrical cords.
4. Keep matches away from young children.
5. Don't keep flammable liquids near a furnace or in other warm places.
6. Don't use gasoline to start fires.
7. Keep towels and other flammable objects away from the stove.
8. Don't throw burning cigarettes in a wastebasket. Always put cigarettes out completely before throwing them away.
9. Always disconnect irons and other electrical appliances after using them.
10. Don't keep oily rags in closed places. They can burst into flames at any time.
11. Keep space heaters away from curtains and furniture.
12. Don't let trash and newspapers pile up.
13. Always have a working smoke detector on each floor of your house.

Practice 1

Circle the number of each precaution which could also apply to work or school.

Practice 2

What fire precaution from page 87 is not being followed in each picture? Write
its number.

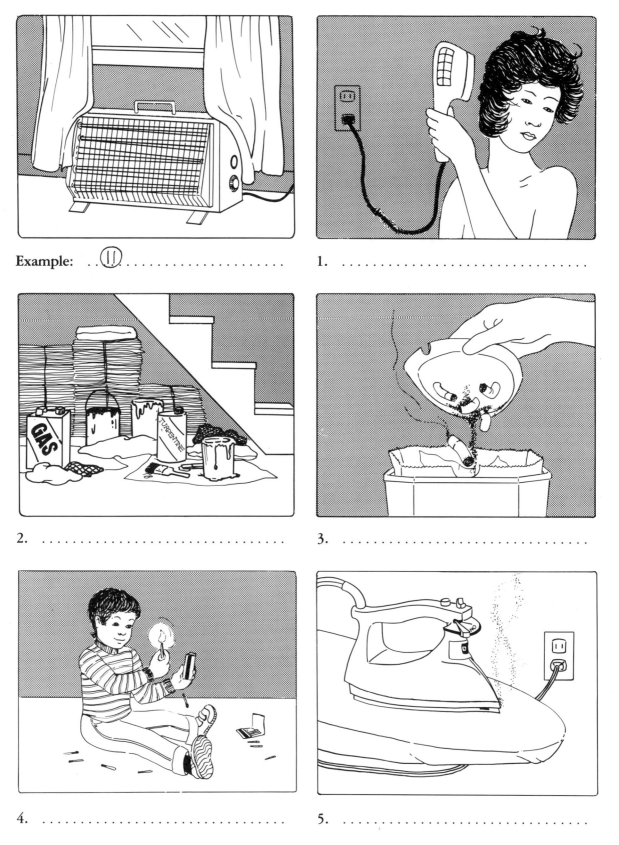

Example: ..⟨11⟩.....................   1. ....

2. ....   3. ....

4. ....   5. ....

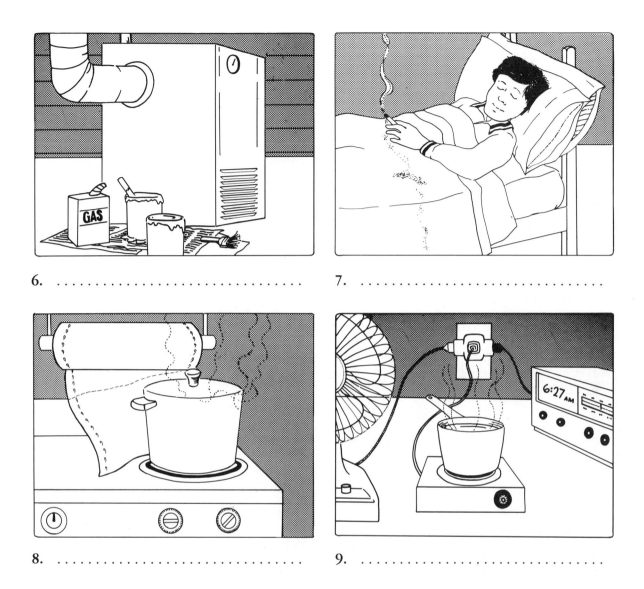

6. . . . .

7. . . . .

8. . . . .

9. . . . .

What to do When There's a Fire

How to put out a small fire

1. Use water or a water fire extinguisher for burning paper, cloth, or wood.
2. A blanket or coat can be used to smother a small fire.
3. For a chemical or electrical fire, use a non-water fire extinguisher.

What to do if a fire cannot be stopped

1. If a fire cannot be put out easily, leave the building immediately.
2. If a door feels hot, don't open it. Find another way out or wait for help.
3. If there is a lot of smoke, crawl on the floor.
4. Don't run if your clothes are on fire. Roll on the floor to put them out.
5. Don't return to the building to rescue other people.
6. Call the fire department immediately.

Using What You've Learned

A. Answer the following questions:

1. Do you have smoke detectors on each floor of your home? _____

   Do they work? _____

2. What is the number of the fire department in your city? _____

   _____

3. Is there a fire extinguisher in your home or at work?

   At home: _____ At work: _____ Are the ex-

   tinguishers water or non-water? _____

   Do you know how to work the fire extinguishers? _____

   Learn to use the fire extinguishers at your school and at work.

4. Do you know what the fire alarm sounds like at your school and at work?

   _____ What should you do when you hear the alarm?

   _____

5. Has your boss or teacher told you which way to leave the building in case of

   fire? _____ If not, ask your teacher or boss to help you find

   the quickest way out.

B. If your workplace or apartment building has special fire precaution rules,
bring the list to class. Your teacher will help you understand these rules if
you have problems.·

C. Make a list of the things you need to do for fire prevention.

1. *Find out about smoke detectors.* _____

2. _____

3. _____

4. _____

5. _____

Apologizing

Conversation 1

It's 8:20 and Linda is late. She is checking in with her supervisor.

Linda: Ms. Garcia, I'm sorry I'm late. My bus was late again.
Ms. Garcia: That's the second time this week, isn't it?
Linda: Yes. I'm going to take an earlier bus from now on.
Ms. Garcia: Good idea, Linda.

Answer these questions:

1. Why did Linda apologize when she got to work?
2. How many times has she been late this week?
3. What is Linda going to do to be on time?

Conversation 2

Tom is helping Sam load boxes on a truck. Tom lets a large box fall on Sam's foot.

Sam: Oh, my foot! Get that box off my foot!
Tom: Oh, I'm sorry! Are you all right?
Sam: Sure. I'll be okay.
Tom: I'm really sorry.
Sam: That's okay. No problem.

Answer these questions:

1. What are Tom and Sam doing?
2. Why did Tom apologize?
3. Is Sam going to be all right?
4. Did Tom apologize once or twice?
5. Is Sam angry at Tom because he dropped the box?

Useful Expressions

1. Apologizing and giving explanations

■ Why aren't you wearing your goggles?
□ I'm sorry. I forgot. It won't happen again.
■ Good.

■ You're late again, Jim.
□ I'm sorry. I missed my bus. I'll get up earlier tomorrow.
■ Good idea.

■ You didn't correct this mistake.
□ I'm sorry. I didn't have time. I'll do it right now.
■ Okay.

■ This floor is still dirty.
□ I'm sorry. I was in a hurry. I'll clean it right now.
■ Thanks.

■ You can't smoke here.
□ I'm sorry. I didn't know.
■ That's okay.

■ I've told you before. You can't wear sandals.
□ I'm sorry. I forgot. It won't happen again.
■ That's good.

Practice 1

Practice apologizing and giving explanations. The first student gives the cue.
The second student's book should be closed.

Example: ■ You can't smoke here.
          □ I'm sorry. I didn't know.

1. You aren't wearing your hard hat.
2. These windows are still dirty.
3. You can't eat your lunch here. I've told you before.
4. Why didn't you correct this mistake?
5. This is the second time you've come back from break late.
6. Why didn't you put your tools away yesterday afternoon?

Practice 2

Think of a time you have apologized and write your own conversation like the
ones above.

■ _____

You: *I'm sorry.* _____

■ _____

2. Apologizing and inquiring if someone is all right

■ Oh, my foot!
□ I'm really sorry. Are you all right?
■ Sure. I'll be okay.

■ Oh, my finger!
□ I'm so sorry. Are you okay?
■ Sure. I'm all right.

3. Apologizing and offering help

You just knocked someone's papers off his desk.

■ I'm	very really	sorry. Let me help you.

□ Thanks.

4. Accepting an apology

■ I'm	very really	sorry.

□ That's | okay. No problem.
all right.

Practice 1

Practice conversations like these with your partner.

Example: *Oh, my foot!*
■ *Oh, my foot!*
□ I'm very sorry. Are you all right?
■ Sure. I'm all right.
□ I'm really sorry.
■ That's okay. No problem.

1. Oh, my hand!
2. Oh, my toe!
3. Oh, my arm!

Practice 2

Write conversations in which you apologize for causing an accident.

Example: ■ I'm very sorry. Let me help you.
□ Thanks.
■ I am really sorry.
□ That's okay. No problem.

1. ■ . . . .
□ . . . .
■ . . . .
□ . . . .

2. ■ . . . .
□ . . . .
■ . . . .
□ . . . .

3. ■ . . . .
□ . . . .
■ . . . .
□ . . . .

Role-plays

Worker A

1. You bump into another worker who is carrying a tray of plastic cups. The tray and the cups fall on the floor.

2. Another worker drops a hammer and it falls on your foot. It hurts a little, but you are okay.

Worker B

Someone bumps into you and knocks the tray of cups you are carrying onto the floor.

You drop a hammer and it falls on another worker's foot.

Worker

3. You are late today. You check in with your supervisor and explain that you missed the bus. You missed the bus yesterday too.

Supervisor

A worker has come late. She was late yesterday too.

Supervisor

4. You asked a worker to clean some tables, but he didn't do a good job.

5. You see a worker eating at her bench and tell her that she can't eat there.

Worker

You were supposed to clean some tables. You were in a hurry and didn't do a good job.

You didn't know that you couldn't eat at your bench.

Talking About Tools and Parts

Conversation 1

Ed is a carpenter. He's working on a table with his co-worker, Mike.

Ed: Can I borrow your screwdriver?
Mike: Sure. Here you go.
Ed: Thanks.

●●●

Ed: Oh no!
Mike: What's up?
Ed: These screws are the wrong size. I'll have to go down to supplies and get some more.
Mike: Say, Ed. I'm short three bolts for this table leg. Can you pick some up for me?
Ed: Sure. No problem.

Conversation 2

Ed goes down to the supply room. Ann is the supply clerk.

Ann: Hi, Ed. What can I do for you?
Ed: I need some screws. These are the wrong size.
Ann: What size do you need?
Ed: One inch.
Ann: How many?
Ed: Give me a box, and a box of half-inch bolts, too.
Ann: Okay. Here you go.
Ed: Thanks.

Write T for true and F for false.

_____ 1. Ed borrows Mike's screwdriver.

_____ 2. Ed's screws are the right size.

_____ 3. Mike needs three more bolts to finish his work.

_____ 4. Ed gets bolts and screws in the supply room.

Useful Expressions

1. Borrowing and returning something

■ Can I borrow your pliers?   □ Sure. Here you are.

■ Thanks.

●●●

(Returning the pliers.)

■ | Thanks for the pliers.   □ | You're welcome.
  | Here are your pliers. Thanks. | Anytime.

Practice

A. Look at the pictures on page 99 and tell your teacher the names of the tools that you know. Then ask about the ones that are new to you.

B. Look at each picture and practice borrowing and returning tools with your partner.

Example: ■ Can I borrow your screwdriver?
          □ Sure.
          ■ Thanks.

●●●

          ■ Thanks for the screwdriver.
          □ You're welcome.

C. Now write the name of each tool under the correct picture.

screwdriver	electric drill
hammer	wrench
saw	Phillips screwdriver
pliers	needle-nosed pliers

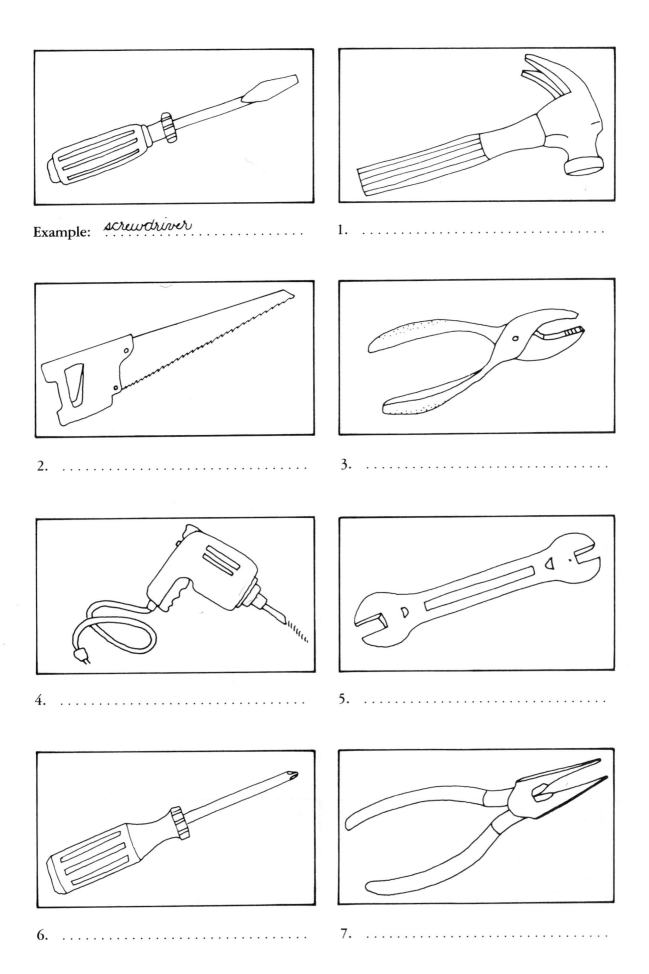

Example: *screwdriver* . . . .

1. . . . .

2. . . . .

3. . . . .

4. . . . .

5. . . . .

6. . . . .

7. . . . .

2. Requesting missing parts

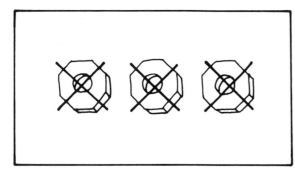

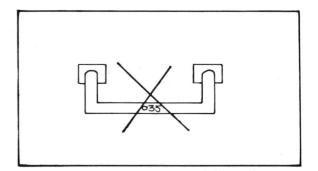

■ I'm missing three bolts.

■ I'm short part #035.

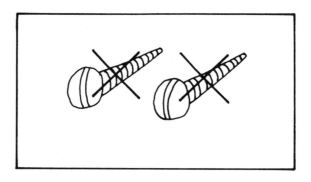

■ I need two screws.

Practice

Look at the pictures and request the parts you are missing.

Example:
■ Can I help you?
□ Yes. I'm short two one-inch screws.
■ Here you are.
□ Thanks.

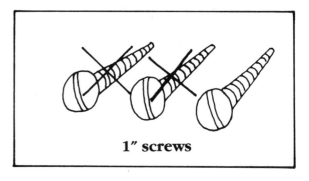

1″ screws

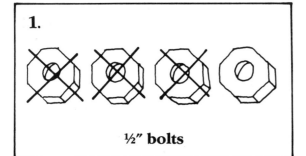

1.

½″ bolts

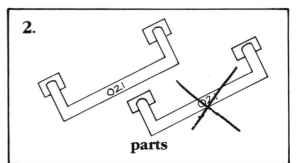

2.

parts

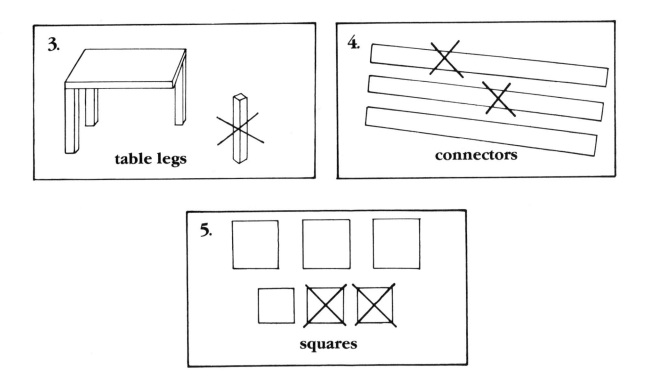

3. table legs

4. connectors

5. squares

3. Requesting tools and describing defects

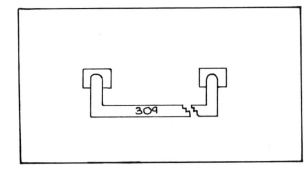

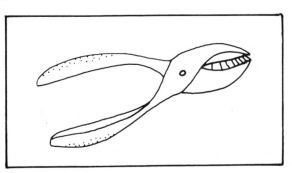

- ■ I need part #309.
  This one is cracked.

- ■ I need a pliers.
  This one is broken.

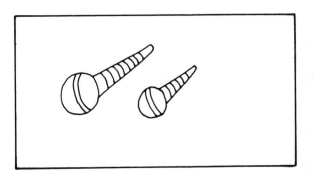

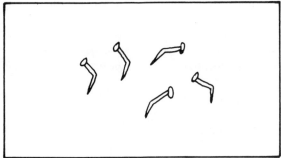

- ■ I need a one-inch screw.
  This one is the wrong size.

- ■ I need some nails.
  These are bent.

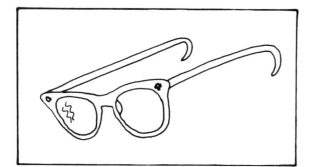

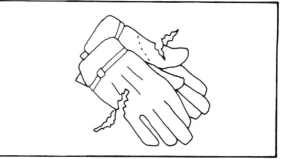

■ I need some safety glasses.
  These are scratched.

■ I need some gloves.
  These are torn.

Practice

Look at the pictures above and practice conversations like the following. While you are practicing, cover the sentences next to the pictures.

Example:

■ What can I do for you?

□ I need some *gloves. These are torn.*

■ Here you are.

Training Exercise

Note to the teacher: Complete instructions for leading this training exercise appear in the *Teacher's Manual*.

Note to the student: You will need your envelope of parts to do this exercise. Check the parts you have against the Parts List and record any missing or defective parts. If any parts are defective, explain the defect. Remember to ask your teacher for help if there is anything you don't understand.

PARTS LIST			
Item Name	**Color**	**Part #**	**Qnty.**
large square	black	021	3
large square	gray	031	3
large square	white	041	3
small square	gray	03	3
small square	white	04	3
long connector	white	06	1
short connector	white	05	2

MISSING AND DEFECTIVE PARTS			
Part #	Description	Circle One	
		missing	defective
		missing	defective
		missing	defective
		missing	defective

Role-plays

Student A

When you have completed the parts list above, go to the supply room and ask for any parts that you are missing. Also report any defective parts and ask for them, too.

Student B

You are the attendant in the supply room. When a worker comes to you, you politely ask what he needs.

Understanding W-4 Forms

W-4 Forms

This is a W-4 form. You must fill out this form so your employer knows how much federal and state income tax to take out of your paycheck. The amount of money the government will take out of your check depends on how much money you make and whom you support.

Form **W-4** (Rev January 1984)	Department of the Treasury—Internal Revenue Service **Employee's Withholding Allowance Certificate**	OMB No 1545-0010

1 Type or print your full name
Helen Wolff

2 Your social security number
328-41-3371

Home address (number and street or rural route)
2126 Grayto

3 Marital Status
☐ Single ☒ Married
☐ Married, but withhold at higher Single rate
Note: If married, but legally separated, or spouse is a nonresident alien, check the Single box.

City or town, State, and ZIP code
Detroit, Michigan   48290

4 Total number of allowances you are claiming (from line F of the worksheet on page 2) *3*

5 Additional amount, if any, you want deducted from each pay . . . . $

6 I claim exemption from withholding because (see instructions and check boxes below that apply):

a ☐ Last year I did not owe any Federal income tax and had a right to a full refund of **ALL** income tax withheld, **AND**

b ☐ This year I do not expect to owe any Federal income tax and expect to have a right to a full refund of **ALL** income tax withheld. If both a and b apply, enter the year effective and "EXEMPT" here ▶   Year

c If you entered "EXEMPT" on line 6b, are you a full-time student? . . . . ☐ Yes ☐ No

Under penalties of perjury, I certify that I am entitled to the number of withholding allowances claimed on this certificate, or if claiming exemption from withholding, that I am entitled to claim the exempt status

Employee's signature ▶ *Helen Wolff*   Date ▶ *October 2*, 19 *85*

7 Employer's name and address (**Employer: Complete 7, 8, and 9 only if sending to IRS**)   **8** Office code   **9** Employer identification number

Allowances: The government gives you allowances or credits.
1. You get allowances for the people you support, including yourself.
2. And you also get extra allowances for the people you support who are blind or 65 or over.

For each allowance you have, the government will withhold (take out) less money from your paycheck. You write the number of allowances you have on line 1 of the W-4 form.

Exemptions: You can also be exempt from paying taxes. This is called "exempt from withholding." This means that the government cannot take any money out of your paycheck because you don't make enough money to be taxed. You can write *exempt* on your W-4 if you didn't owe taxes last year and you won't owe any taxes this year. If you work part-time, you will probably be exempt.

Practice

As you read about allowances, write down the correct numbers for yourself.

_____ 1. You get 1 allowance for yourself.

_____ 2. You get 1 allowance if you are 65 or over.

_____ 3. You get 1 allowance if you are blind.

_____ 4. You get 1 allowance for your spouse if he/she doesn't work.

_____ 5. You get 1 allowance if your spouse is 65 or over and doesn't work.

_____ 6. You get 1 allowance if your spouse is blind and doesn't work.

_____ 7. You get 1 allowance for each child if your support is 50% or more.

_____ 8. You get 1 allowance for each parent if your support is 50% or more.

_____ 9. You get 1 extra allowance if the parent you support is blind or 65 or over.

_____ 10. You get 1 allowance for each brother or sister if your support is 50% or more.

_____ **TOTAL**

Note: If your spouse is working and is putting allowances on his/her W-4, you cannot put the same allowances on your W-4 form.

Filling Out a W-4 Form

Follow the steps below and fill out the W-4 form on page 106 for yourself.

1. Print your name and address.
2. Write your social security number.
3. Check *married* or *single*. If you are separated or divorced, check *single*.
4. If you are not exempt, write the number of allowances you get at the end of line 4.
5. Skip line 5.
6. If you are exempt:
   Write the year for which you are exempt.
   Print the word *exempt* after the black arrow.

Check boxes 6a and 6b.

If you are a full-time student, check box 6c.

7. Sign your name and write the date.

Note: Do not write in boxes 7, 8, and 9.

Form **W-4** (Rev January 1984)	Department of the Treasury—Internal Revenue Service **Employee's Withholding Allowance Certificate**	OMB No 1545-0010

1 Type or print your full name		2 Your social security number

Home address (number and street or rural route)

City or town, State, and ZIP code

3 Marital Status
- [ ] Single   [ ] Married
- [ ] Married, but withhold at higher Single rate

Note: If married, but legally separated, or spouse is a nonresident alien, check the Single box.

4 Total number of allowances you are claiming (from line F of the worksheet on page 2) . . . .

5 Additional amount, if any, you want deducted from each pay . . . . $

6 I claim exemption from withholding because (see instructions and check boxes below that apply):

   a [ ] Last year I did not owe any Federal income tax and had a right to a full refund of **ALL** income tax withheld, **AND**

   b [ ] This year I do not expect to owe any Federal income tax and expect to have a right to a full refund of   Year   **ALL** income tax withheld. If both a and b apply, enter the year effective and ''EXEMPT'' here ▶

   c   If you entered ''EXEMPT'' on line 6b, are you a full-time student? . . . . [ ]Yes [ ]No

Under penalties of perjury, I certify that I am entitled to the number of withholding allowances claimed on this certificate, or if claiming exemption from withholding, that I am entitled to claim the exempt status

Employee's signature ▶   Date ▶   , 19

7 Employer's name and address (**Employer: Complete 7, 8, and 9 only if sending to IRS**) | 8 Office code | 9 Employer identification number

---

Practice

Figure out how many allowances Mee Vang should get and then fill out the W-4 form on the next page for her.

Mee Vang is a seamstress. She is 55 years old and married. Her husband is 60 years old, and he does not work. They have eight children, but they only support three now. How many allowances should she put down?

Mee Vang: _____

Spouse (husband): _____

Children: _____

Parents: _____

Brothers/Sisters: _____

TOTAL: _____

Mee Vang
146 Dale St.
St. Paul, MN 55102
Soc. Sec. #447-79-3688

Form **W-4** (Rev. January 1984)	Department of the Treasury—Internal Revenue Service **Employee's Withholding Allowance Certificate**	OMB No. 1545-0010

1 Type or print your full name

2 Your social security number

Home address (number and street or rural route)

City or town, State, and ZIP code

3 Marital Status

☐ Single ☐ Married
☐ Married, but withhold at higher Single rate
Note: If married, but legally separated, or spouse is a nonresident alien, check the Single box.

4 Total number of allowances you are claiming (from line F of the worksheet on page 2) . . . .

5 Additional amount, if any, you want deducted from each pay . . . . $

6 I claim exemption from withholding because (see instructions and check boxes below that apply):
  a ☐ Last year I did not owe any Federal income tax and had a right to a full refund of **ALL** income tax withheld, **AND**
  b ☐ This year I do not expect to owe any Federal income tax and expect to have a right to a full refund of **ALL** income tax withheld. If both a and b apply, enter the year effective and "EXEMPT" here . . ▶ Year
  c If you entered "EXEMPT" on line 6b, are you a full-time student? . . . . ☐ Yes ☐ No

Under penalties of perjury, I certify that I am entitled to the number of withholding allowances claimed on this certificate, or if claiming exemption from withholding, that I am entitled to claim the exempt status

Employee's signature ▶   Date ▶   , 19

7 Employer's name and address (**Employer: Complete 7, 8, and 9 only if sending to IRS**)

8 Office code

9 Employer identification number

In the U.S.

Phonthan and Pring work for the same company. Pring is married and has three children. Phonthan is single. They are both mechanics, and they make the same hourly wage. During the last pay period, they both worked the same number of hours, but Phonthan's take-home pay was $48 less than Pring's. There was no mistake on the checks. Can you explain why the checks were different?

1. Who has more allowances on his W-4 form?

2. Who will have more money deducted from his gross pay?

7

Talking About the Weather

Conversation

Martha and Susan are walking into work on a very cold day.

Susan: Isn't this weather terrible?
Martha: It sure is.
Susan: My car wouldn't start this morning.
Martha: Oh, no! How did you get to work?
Susan: I took the bus and was I cold!
Martha: How cold is it?
Susan: About 5 below zero.
Martha: Is it going to snow?
Susan: Yeah, I heard ten inches by tonight.
Martha: That's awful!
Susan: You can say that again!
Martha: Okay, Susan. See you at break.
Susan: See you. Keep warm!

Write T for true or F for false.

_____ 1. The weather is terrible today.

_____ 2. The temperature is above zero.

_____ 3. It isn't going to snow any more.

_____ 4. Martha and Susan think the weather is awful.

_____ 5. Martha couldn't start her car this morning.

_____ 6. Susan was cold waiting for the bus.

Useful Expressions

1. Starting a conversation about the weather

■	Isn't this	weather	beautiful?	□	It sure is!
			terrible?		You can say that again!
		smog terrible?			
	Isn't it	hot	today?		
		cold			
		humid			

Practice

Practice conversations like the examples.

Examples:

smog terrible
■ Isn't this *smog terrible?*
□ It sure is.

hot today
■ Isn't it *hot today?*
□ You can say that again.

1. weather great
2. heat awful
3. sun wonderful

4. cold today
5. windy today
6. humid today

2. Talking about the weather

■ What's the temperature? □ It's 75. ■ That's not too bad.

■ How hot is it? □ It's 99. ■ That's hot!

■ How cold is it? □ It's 5 below. ■ That's cold!

■ Is it going to snow?   □ | Yes. About   ■ | That's awful.
                              | ten inches. |
                              | I don't think so. | That's good.

■ Is it going to rain?   □ | I hope not.   ■ Me too.
                              | I hope so.

Practice

Practice these cold and hot weather conversations with your partner.

hot	cold
■ Isn't it hot today?	■ Isn't it cold today?
□ It sure is!	□ You can say that again!
■ What's the temperature?	■ How cold is it?
□ About 95.	□ About five below.
■ 95! That's hot!	■ That's cold!
□ Is it going to rain?	□ Is it going to snow?
■ I hope so.	■ Yes. About eight inches.
□ Me too.	□ That's terrible.

3. Talking about transportation problems

A. ■ | I couldn't start | this morning.   □ What did you do?
        | my car |
        | My car wouldn't |
        | start |

   ■ | I jumped it.
        | I took the bus.
        | A friend drove me.

B. ■ | I got stuck | this morning.   □ What did you do?
        | My car got stuck |

   ■ | Someone pushed it.
        | I shoveled it out.

C. ■ | I missed the bus.   □ Oh, no! How did you get to
        | My bus never came.   work?
        | My bus didn't stop.

   ■ | I walked.
        | A friend drove me.
        | I waited for the next bus.

Practice

Practice conversations like those above with your partner.

Example: My car wouldn't start this morning.
- ■ My car wouldn't start this morning.
- □ What did you do?
- ■ I took the bus.

1. I got stuck this morning.
2. I couldn't start my car this morning.
3. I missed the bus this morning.
4. My bus never came this morning.
5. My car got stuck.
6. My bus didn't stop.

Role-plays

Student A	Student B
1. It's hot. You don't like the hot weather. It's 90° today.	It's hot. You missed the bus and walked to work. You ask how hot it is.
2. It's winter and very cold. You ask how cold it is, and you want to know if it's going to snow.	It's snowing and very cold. It's 2°. There will be 8 inches of snow by tonight. Your car wouldn't start. You took the bus.

Using What You've Learned

Remember that talking about the weather is a good conversation starter. At work this week, talk to someone about the weather. Tell your classmates what happened.

Understanding Schedule Changes

Conversation 1

Tou makes salad in a restaurant. She usually works from 8:00 to 5:00. Tou is cleaning up to go home when her supervisor, Janet, comes by at 4:30.

Janet: Tou, could I talk to you a minute?
Tou: Sure, Janet.
Janet: Tou, I really have my hands full tonight. Could you work late this evening?
Tou: I'm sorry, I don't understand.
Janet: I need you to stay and work until about 9:00.
Tou: Oh, I see. That's fine. I can stay.
Janet: Good. By the way, remember to check the work schedule tomorrow. There'll be some changes this week.
Tou: Okay. I'll remember.
Janet: Thanks for staying, Tou.
Tou: No problem.

Write T for true and F for false.

_____ 1. Tou's supervisor wants to talk to her.

_____ 2. There is a lot of work tonight.

_____ 3. Janet wants Tou to come to work at 9:00 tomorrow.

_____ 4. Tou says she can't stay.

_____ 5. Tou has to check the work schedule tomorrow.

Useful Expressions

1. Answering when you are interrupted

■	Could I talk to you a minute? Can I see you a minute? Do you have a minute?	□	Sure. Sure. What's up?

■	Are you busy right now?	□	No. No. What's up?

Practice

Practice conversations like these.

2. Understanding a request to do extra work

■ I really have my hands full. Could you stay late?
We're really busy. Could you come in early?
There's a lot of work. Could you work the night shift?
We're behind schedule. I need you to stay late.

3. Answering your boss about doing extra work

A. If you are not sure you understand, you can say:
■ I'm sorry. I don't understand.

B. If you can work, you say:
■ Sure. I can do that.
Okay. I can stay late.
No problem. I can come early.

C. If you can't work, you say:
■ I'm sorry. I can't | come early tomorrow.
stay late today.
work then.

Practice

Practice conversations following the example.

Example: *I'm really busy. Can you come in early?* (no)
■ *I'm really busy. Can you come in early?*
□ I'm sorry, I don't understand.
■ *Can you come in early?*
□ *I'm sorry. I can't come in early.*

1. I really have my hands full. Could you stay late? (yes)
2. We're behind schedule. I'd like you to work late. (no)
3. There's a lot of work. Can you work the swing shift? (yes)
4. I'm really busy. I need you to come in early. (yes)

4. Explaining why you can't do extra work

■ | I have an appointment at the doctor.
| I don't have a babysitter.
| I have an evening class.

Practice 1

Repeat the previous practice. Each time, answer that you can't work and then give an excuse.

Practice 2

Listening:

A. Listen to your teacher, then circle the sentence that has the same meaning.

1. a. You can't stay.
    b. There's a lot of work.

2. a. You understand.
    b. You don't understand.

B. Listen to your teacher's questions, then circle the correct response.

3. a. Yes. What can I do for you?
    b. No. What's up?

4. a. No, I can't.
    b. Sure.

5. a. No, I can't come in early.
    b. Sure, I can stay.

6. a. Fine. I can come early.
    b. I can do that.

5. Finding out when you have to do extra work

| ■ Could you come in early? | □ | What time | do you want me to |
| | | When | come? |

■ | At 5:30.
| For the night shift.
| At 6 in the morning.

■ Can you stay late?	□ How long do you	want me to
		stay?
		need me to
		work?

■ | Until 9:30.
| For two more hours.
| For the night shift.

Practice

Practice conversations like these with your teacher or another student.

Examples:

- ■ Can you work late?
- □ Sure. How long do you want me to stay?
- ■ Until 9:30.

- ■ I need you to come in early.
- □ What time do you want me to come in?
- ■ For the day shift.

6. Checking the work schedule

■ Please check the work schedule every day. Remember to check the work schedule.	□ I will. I'll remember.

- ■ Don't forget to check the work schedule.   □ I won't.

Practice 1

Practice conversations like this with your teacher or another student.

- ■ Don't forget to check the work schedule.
- □ I won't.

Practice 2

Practice this conversation with a partner. The person doing role A can read from the book. After each person has practiced role B, write the conversation.

A: _____, can I talk to you a minute?
    (B's name)

B: _____

A: I'm really busy. Can you stay late this afternoon?

B: _____

A: Until 9:30.

B: _____

A: Thanks for staying. And don't forget to check the work schedule.

B: _____

Conversation 2

José is a cook. He usually works the graveyard shift from 9:30 p.m. to 5:30 a.m. His supervisor calls him at home at 3:00 in the afternoon.

José: Hello.

Supervisor: Is José Estrada there?

José: This is José.

Supervisor: José, this is Henry.

José: Henry, what can I do for you?

Supervisor: One of my night workers just got sick. Could you come in early this evening?

José: When do you want me to come in?

Supervisor: For the 5:00 to 9:30 shift.

José: That's fine. I can do that.

Supervisor: That's great. See you later.

José: Bye.

Write T for true and F for false.

_____ 1. José's supervisor called him at home.

_____ 2. José's supervisor wants him to come in early tomorrow.

_____ 3. José is sick and can't go in to work.

_____ 4. Henry wants José to work the 5:00 to 9:30 shift.

_____ 5. José is going to go to work early tonight.

Useful Expressions

Answering the phone

■ Hello.
□ Hello, is Ali there?
■ This is Ali.
□ Ali, this is Pat Sanders.
■ Hi, Pat. What can I do for you?

Practice 1

Practice answering the phone with your teacher or another student.

Practice 2

Practice this conversation with a partner. The person doing role B can read from the book. After each person has practiced role A, write the conversation.

A: Hello.

B: Is _____ there?
          (A's name)

A: _____

B: Hello, _____ . This is _____ .
                                                    (B's name)

A: Hello, _____ . What _____ ?

B: I have my hands full this afternoon. Could you come in early this afternoon?

A: _____

B: At 5:30.

A: _____

B: Thanks. See you at 5:30 then.

A: _____

Role-plays

Student A	Student B
1. You're the boss. You're very busy. You want this worker to stay late. You want him to work until 9:00.	You don't understand at first. You can work late. You want to know how long you'll have to work.
2. You are the foreman. You call a worker to come in early at 7:00. You remind her to check the work schedule.	You are at home. Your boss calls. You can go to work early. You want to know what time your boss wants you to come in.
3. You're the supervisor. You're behind schedule. You want a worker to stay and work the 5:30 to 9:30 shift.	You're at work. It's time to go home. You can't stay because you don't have a babysitter for your children.

Training Exercise

Note to the teacher: Complete instructions for leading your students in this training exercise are in the *Teacher's Manual.*

Note to the students: In this exercise you will practice following written instructions. You will need your envelope of parts and the board on page 69. Your teacher will be your lead worker and will answer any questions you have.

Understanding Benefits

Benefits

When you apply for a job, you not only need to find out how much your salary will be, but also what benefits you will get. Benefits are not the same at all companies. It is also important to remember that part-time workers don't usually get full benefits. Read and discuss the following benefits with your teacher.

Paid vacation: Workers get a certain number of paid vacation days a year. They usually get longer vacations if they have worked for the company for several years.

Paid holidays: Workers get a certain number of holidays, such as Christmas and Thanksgiving, for which they are paid.

Sick days: If workers are sick, they can take a day off and still get paid. The number of sick days workers get a year varies from company to company.

Health insurance: Workers get help from their companies to pay for health insurance for themselves and their families.

Maternity or paternity leave: Companies allow mothers or fathers to stay home and take care of their newborn babies for a few months. Usually workers are not paid for this time.

Unemployment compensation: If workers lose their jobs, they receive a percentage of their salary to live on until they can find employment again. If a worker has only worked at a company for a short time, he may not get unemployment compensation.

Workers' compensation: If workers get hurt on the job, they receive money to live on until they can work again.

Retirement pension: Usually when people are about 65 years old, they stop working. This is called retirement. For every year that an employee works, the company saves a certain amount of money for the employee to live on when she retires. This money is called a retirement pension. At some companies both the employer and the employee put money in the pension.

Write T for true and F for false.

_____ 1. Part-time workers usually get full-time benefits.

_____ 2. Workers who have worked for a company for five years get more paid vacation days than new workers.

_____ 3. Workers are not paid for holidays.

_____ 4. If workers miss work because they are sick, they will not be paid.

_____ 5. When women take maternity leave, they are usually paid their salary.

_____ 6. If workers have health insurance, they will get help with their medical expenses.

_____ 7. Some companies help workers pay for health insurance.

_____ 8. Workers' compensation pays workers if they are hurt on the job and can't work.

_____ 9. A pension is money used by workers when they retire.

_____ 10. Unemployment compensation pays a full salary to workers when they lose their jobs.

Using What You've Learned

If you are working, complete this checklist of benefits for yourself. If you are not working, interview a friend about his or her benefits, and then fill out the checklist.

1. Do you work | full-time? _____ yes _____ no

                | part-time? _____ yes _____ no

2. Do you have paid vacation days? _____ yes _____ no

   How many? _____

3. Do you have paid holidays? _____ yes _____ no

   How many? _____

4. Do you have sick days? _____ yes _____ no

   How many? _____

5. Do you have health insurance? _____ yes _____ no

   You pay _____ .

   The company pays _____ .

6. Do you have a pension plan? _____ yes _____ no

7. Will your company give you maternity/paternity _____ yes _____ no

   leave?

8. Have you ever collected unemployment compensation? _____ yes _____ no

9. Have you ever collected workers' compensation? _____ yes _____ no

Talking About Your Weekend

Conversation 1

Olga is talking to her friend Luz on Monday morning.

Olga: Morning, Luz.

Luz: Hi, Olga. How're you doing?

Olga: Not bad. How was your weekend?

Luz: Really nice. I went to a Bruce Lee movie, and on Sunday some friends
came over.

Olga: Sounds like fun.

Luz: Did you have a nice weekend, Olga?

Olga: Not really. My kids had the flu.

Luz: That's no fun. Are they better now?

Olga: Yes, a lot better, thanks.

Luz: Time to punch in.

Olga: Right. See you at break.

Write T for true and F for false.

_____ 1. Luz had a nice weekend.

_____ 2. Olga had a nice weekend, too.

_____ 3. Luz saw a Bruce Lee movie.

_____ 4. Olga's children had the flu.

_____ 5. Olga's kids aren't better yet.

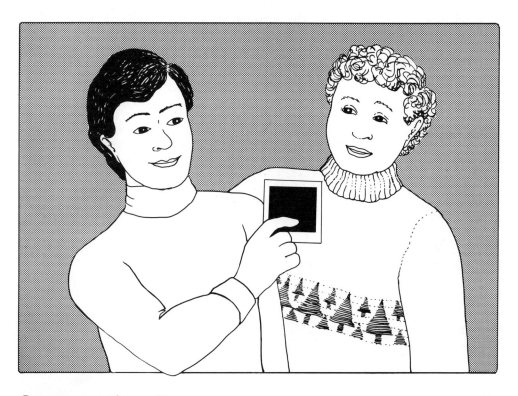

Conversation 2

Ali and Dan are chatting at lunch.

Dan: You look happy, Ali. What's up?
Ali: My wife just had a baby.
Dan: Congratulations, Ali! A girl or a boy?
Ali: A girl.
Dan: That's great. I'm so happy for you.

Write T for true and F for false.

_____ 1. Ali looks happy.

_____ 2. Ali is happy because he has a new job.

_____ 3. People say *congratulations* when they hear good news.

_____ 4. Ali's wife had a baby boy.

_____ 5. Dan is happy for Ali.

Useful Expressions

1. Talking about your weekend

A. ■ How was your weekend?

_____   _____

☐ | Really nice. I took my kids   ☐ | Not very good. I was sick.
      to the zoo.   Boring. I cleaned all weekend.
  | Great. I visited some friends.

■ | That's nice.   ■ | Oh, that's too bad.
  | Sounds like a good time. | That's no fun.

B. ■ Did you have a nice weekend?
    ☐ | Yes, I went to a movie.
      | No, I was sick.

C. ■ What did you do this weekend?
    ☐ I | stayed home.
       | visited friends.

Practice 1

Decide if the weekend was good or bad and then practice conversations like this with your partner.

Example: *I was sick.*
■ How was your weekend?
☐ Not very good. *I was sick.*
■ That's no fun.

1. My kids were sick.
2. I went to Boston.
3. I broke my arm.
4. My sister got married.
5. I went to a party.

Practice 2

Write five things you did last weekend.

1. _____
2. _____
3. _____
4. _____
5. _____

Use your answers to practice conversations like these.

- What did you do this weekend?
- ☐ I went to a party.
- That sounds like fun.

- Did you have a nice weekend?
- ☐ No. My children were sick.
- That's too bad.

2. Asking if someone is feeling better

- I had the flu.

☐ Are you | better now?
| feeling better now?

- Yes, | much better now.
  | a little better.
  No, I'm still sick.

Practice

Practice conversations like this with your partner.

Example: *the flu*
- How was your weekend?
- ☐ Not very good. I had *the flu*.
- That's too bad.
- ☐ Are you better now?
- Yes, a little better.

1. a cold
2. a sore throat
3. a bad stomachache

3. Responding to special news
- My wife had a baby.
- ☐ Congratulations! A boy or a girl?
- A girl.
- ☐ That's wonderful!

- Ann and I are getting married.
- ☐ Congratulations! When's the wedding?
- On June 21st.
- ☐ That's great!

Practice

Practice conversations like those above with a partner.

Role-plays

Student A

1. You ask how your friend's weekend was. Your weekend was bad. You had a bad cough all weekend. Your cough is still not better, and you're going to the doctor this afternoon.

2. You ask a friend how his weekend was. Your weekend was great. You went fishing and caught three fish.

3. You ask a friend how his weekend was.

4. You ask your friend why she looks so happy.

Student B

Your weekend was good. You had a birthday party for your son. It was fun. You ask your friend how her weekend was.

Your weekend was bad. Your children were sick. They had bad colds, but they're feeling better now. You ask your friend how her weekend was.

You are very happy because your wife had a baby boy.

You are very happy becasue you are going to get married on the 21st of this month.

Understanding Procedure Changes

Conversation 1

George is a secretary. He's doing some filing when his supervisor comes by.

Supervisor: Are you finished?
George: No, not quite.
Supervisor: How long will it take?
George: About five minutes more.
Supervisor: Okay. When you finish those, I want you to put these cards in alphabetical order, using the last names, and then make a list.
George: You want the cards in alphabetical order, using the last names.
Supervisor: That's right.
George: And what was the last thing?
Supervisor: I want a list of the names.
George: I see. How many copies?
Supervisor: Just one.
George: Good, Mr. Anderson. I'll get to it right now.

Write T for true and F for false.

_____ 1. George is a secretary.

_____ 2. He has just finished filing.

_____ 3. George's supervisor wants him to put the cards in alphabetical order.

_____ 4. George repeats what his boss tells him to do.

_____ 5. George will start the new work in about 30 minutes.

Conversation 2

Maria is a salad worker. A waitress needs her help.

Maria: Hi, Lisa.

Lisa: Maria, I'm sorry. You'll have to change this salad. I need a salad without tomatoes. You'll have to substitute cucumbers.

Maria: I'm not sure I understand.

Lisa: There's a man who doesn't want tomatoes. You'll have to make one with cucumbers and no tomatoes.

Maria: Oh, I see. Cucumbers but no tomatoes on this one.

Lisa: That's right.

Maria: Okay. I'll fix it right now.

Lisa: Thanks.

Write T for true and F for false.

_____ 1. Maria is a waitress.

_____ 2. Maria is making salad with tomatoes.

_____ 3. The waitress asks Maria to change something.

_____ 4. Maria doesn't understand at first.

_____ 5. Maria is going to change the salad right now.

Useful Expressions

1. Saying when you'll be finished

■ Are you finished?	☐ No, not yet. Yes, I am.
■ Aren't you finished yet? (Your boss thinks you should be finished.)	☐ Sorry. I'm not quite done. Yes, I just finished.
■ When will you be finished?	☐ In about five minutes. a minute.
■ How long will it take?	☐ About five minutes more. an hour. I'm not sure.

Practice

Practice conversations like those above with your partner.

Example: ■ *Aren't you finished yet?*
        □ I'm sorry. I'm not quite done.
        ■ When will you be finished?
        □ In about five minutes.

1. Are you finished yet?
2. Aren't you done?
3. How long will it take?
4. When will you be done?

2. Understanding when to do a job

■ | After you sweep, clear the tables.
  | When you finish sweeping, clear the tables.

■ Before you sweep, clear the tables.

■ Before you finish sweeping, clear the tables.

Practice

Listening: Look at the pictures. (This time the pictures are not always in the correct order.) Then listen to the instructions and place a check (√) next to the activity that comes first.

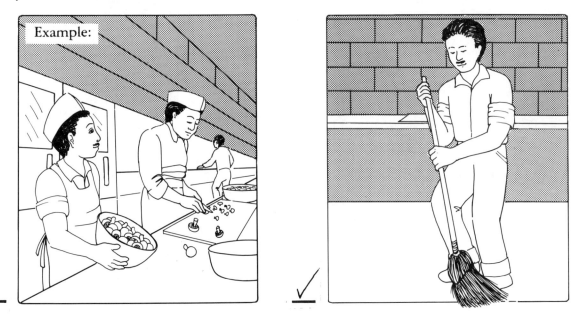

Example:

1.

2.

3.

4. ___   ___

3. Repeating instructions to make sure you understand

■ I want you to sweep the kitchen, clean the stove, and put the dishes away.

_____   _____

☐ Sweep, clean the stove, and put   ☐ Sweep, clean the stove, and what
   the dishes away?   was the last thing?
■ Right.   ■ Put the dishes away.
☐ Okay.   ☐ Okay.

4. Saying when you'll do your work

■ | I'll do it right now.
  | I'll start it now.
  | I'll do it in about ten minutes.

Practice

Practice conversations with your partner. Follow the example.

Example:
clean the sink
clean the tub
mop the bathroom floor

■ I want you to *clean the sink and the tub* and *mop the bathroom floor*.
☐ *Clean the sink and the tub* and what was the last thing?
■ *Mop the bathroom floor*.
☐ Okay. I'll do it right now.

1. change the beds
   vacuum the floor
   dust the furniture

2. type these letters
   file these papers
   attend a meeting

3. put these cards in alphabetical order
   make a list of the names
   take the list to personnel

5. Asking information questions

■ I want three squares in column B.
□ How many?
■ Three.
□ Okay.

_____

□ What color?	■ Black.
□ What size?	■ Small.
□ Where?	■ At B2.
□ How many?	■ Two.
□ (In) what column?	■ Column B.
□ (In) what line?	■ Line 2.

Practice

Practice conversations with your partner. Follow the example.

Example:
■ Put a *small* square at C2.
□ What size?
■ *Small.*
□ Okay.

1. Put a gray square at C2.
2. Put a black square in line five.
3. Put three gray squares in column C.
4. Put two squares in column B.
5. Put a large square at D3.

Training Exercise

Note to the teacher: Complete instructions for leading your students in this training exercise are in the *Teacher's Manual.*

Note to the student: In this exercise, you will practice dealing with a change in the work procedure. You will need to use your envelope of parts and the board on page 69. Get your materials ready, and then follow your teacher's instructions carefully.

—— **Assembly Plan A**

BOARD # _____

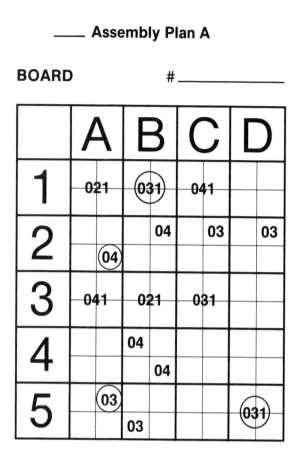

	A	B	C	D
1	021	(031)	041	
2		04 / (04)	03	03
3	041	021	031	
4		04 / 04		
5		(03) / 03		(031)

1. Record your board number on the assembly plan.
2. Use the plan to complete your board.
3. Connections
   • Use 05 to connect 04(A2) and 03(A5).
   • Use 06 to connect 031 (B1) and 031(D5).
4. Have lead worker check your board.

5. _____
   (signature)

—— **Assembly Plan B**

BOARD # _____

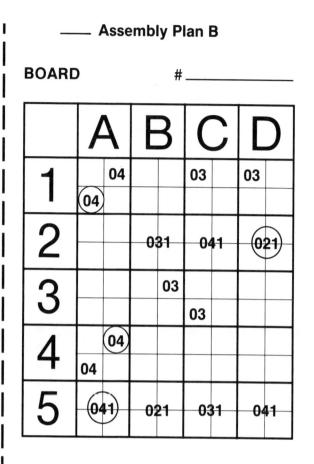

	A	B	C	D
1	04 / (04)	04	03	03
2		031	041	(021)
3		03 / 03		
4	04 / (04)			
5	(041)	021	031	041

1. Record your board number on the assembly plan.
2. Use the plan to complete your board.
3. Connections
   • Use 05 to connect 04(A1) and 04(A4).
   • Use 06 to connect 041(A5) and 021(D2).
4. Have lead worker check your work.

5. _____
   (signature)

(FOLD HERE)

In the U.S.

Kate is an assembler. She does soldering and wiring. She likes to learn new things. If someone is absent, Kate doesn't mind doing different jobs when her supervisor asks her. Lucille is an assembler, too. She only knows how to do soldering. She doesn't like to do different jobs, and her supervisor never asks her. Last week one of these workers got a new job with higher pay. Who do you think got the job? Why?

Understanding Health Insurance

Health Insurance

Because going to the doctor and staying in the hospital are so expensive in the U.S., it is very important to have health insurance. People buy insurance, and when they have doctor or hospital bills, the insurance company pays part or all of the costs. Here are some questions you should ask when you buy health insurance.

How much will the insurance cost, and how often do I have to pay?
The money you pay for insurance is called a premium. Some insurance premiums are paid twice or four times a year; other premiums are paid every month. The cost of insurance varies from company to company.

Does the insurance policy give full or partial coverage (payment for expenses)?
Some policies do not pay 100 percent of the medical costs. For example, the insurance company may only pay 80 percent of the costs and you would have to pay the other 20 percent.

Does the policy have a deductible and how much is it?
A deductible is that part of your medical expenses for the year which you must pay before your insurance company will begin to repay you. Many policies have a $100 deductible for individuals. If your policy has a $100 deductible, you must pay the first $100 of your expenses each year. Your insurance company would then cover all other medical expenses that year, fully or in part, depending on the terms of your policy.

What will the insurance pay for?
There are two main kinds of health insurance: Hospitalization Insurance and Comprehensive Insurance.
1. Hospitalization insurance is the cheapest insurance you can buy. This insurance will help you pay your medical bills if you have to go to the hospital. It will pay for your room, surgery, nursing care, and other hospital costs. This kind of insurance does not pay for visits to the doctor or medicine.

2. Comprehensive insurance is usually more expensive than hospitalization insurance. This kind of insurance pays for hospital care, and it also pays for you when you go to the doctor, buy medicine, or stay in a nursing home. There is a new kind of comprehensive insurance called an HMO (Health Maintenance Organization) plan. When you belong to an HMO clinic, you pay a monthly fee and there is no deductible. As long as you use HMO doctors and hospitals, you have no other payments, except for medicine, which is very inexpensive.

Does the insurance policy have a lot of paperwork?
Some insurance plans are very complicated and require that you fill out many forms every time you send in a claim (request for payment) to the insurance company. Other plans are easier. For example, if you belong to an HMO, you fill out an application form, pay a monthly fee, and all your hospital and doctor bills are automatically paid for.

Using What You've Learned

A. If you are working, find out about your health insurance. Then answer the following questions and complete the insurance checklist. If you are not working, complete the exercise by interviewing someone about his or her health insurance.

1. What kind of insurance do you have?

_____ Hospitalization insurance

_____ Comprehensive insurance

_____ Health Maintenance Organization

2. Does your employer help you pay for your insurance? _____

How much does your company pay? _____

How much do you pay? _____

3. Do you have to pay a deductible? _____

How much is it? _____

4. Check the kinds of care that are paid for by your insurance.

_____ visits to the doctor	_____ nursing
_____ prescription drugs	_____ ambulance
_____ nursing home	_____ emergency room
_____ eye exams	_____ lab work
_____ dental care	_____ X-rays
_____ hospital room	_____ _____
_____ surgery	_____ _____

B. Practice filling out this insurance application form. If you have any insurance forms from your workplace, bring them to class and your teacher will help you fill them out.

■■ GROUP
■■ HEALTH
■■ INC.

MEDICAL/DENTAL ENROLLMENT FORM

2829 University Avenue SE
Minneapolis, Minnesota 55414

COVERAGE APPLYING FOR:	☐ Medical Coverage ☐ Employee Only ☐ Employee and 1 Dependent ☐ Employee and 2 or more Dependents	☐ Dental Coverage ☐ Employee Only ☐ Employee and 1 Dependent ☐ Employee and 2 or more Dependents	☐ Single ☐ Married ☐ Widowed ☐ Divorced

EMPLOYEE: Last Name	First Name	M.I.	Sex	Date of Birth Mo. Day Year	Social Security Number

LIST ALL ELIGIBLE DEPENDENTS: Last Name	First Name	M.I.	Sex	Date of Birth Mo. Day Year	Soc. Sec. No.	Relationship

EMPLOYEE'S ADDRESS:

Street Address	Home Phone
(County) City State Zip	Work Phone

Have you or any member(s) of your family previously been members of Group Health, Inc. ☐ Yes ☐ No
If yes, please indicate the name(s) and member numbers below:

Member Name(s)   Member Number(s)

_____   _____

_____   _____

MEDICAL DENTAL CENTER: If you or family members wish to select a Group Health Medical and or Dental Center please write your choices below. If not, you will be assigned to the Medical and or Dental Center closest to your home.

Name(s)   Medical and or Dental Center

_____   _____

_____   _____

_____   _____

If changing health plans, check previous health plan: ☐ Indemnity insurance plan ☐ Another HMO Name: _____

EMPLOYEE'S SIGNATURE: _____ Date: _____

Describing Past Work and Education

Conversation

Kim works in the mailroom of a large company. She and Bill find a table in the cafeteria and sit down to have lunch.

Bill: Let's sit here.
Kim: Okay.
Bill: Kim, what did you do in Vietnam?
Kim: I worked in a bank.
Bill: What kind of work did you do?
Kim: I was a teller.
Bill: Is this your first job in the U.S.?
Kim: No. Before this I worked in a Vietnamese restaurant.
Bill: How long did you work there?

Kim: About three months.
Bill: Do you like this job better?
Kim: Yes. I like the work better, and the pay is better, too.
Bill: And you're learning a lot of English here, too.
Kim: Yes, that's the best part.
Bill: Your English is really improving.
Kim: Thanks, Bill. I'm studying English at night, you know.
Bill: That's great. Did you study English before you came here?
Kim: Just three months in the Philippines. In Vietnam I studied French.
Bill: How many years did you study French?
Kim: Oh, about six years.
Bill: Boy, your French must be good.
Kim: It's pretty good. How about you, Bill? What languages do you speak?
Bill: Me? I only know English.
Kim: You could study French at night school, you know.
Bill: You're right, I could.

Write T for true and F for false.

_____ 1. Kim is working in a restaurant now.

_____ 2. She has had two jobs in the U.S.

_____ 3. She was a bank teller in Vietnam.

_____ 4. Kim's pay is better now.

_____ 5. Kim studied English for six years.

_____ 6. Kim speaks French.

_____ 7. Kim is learning a lot of English at her new job.

_____ 8. Bill speaks French, too.

Useful Expressions

1. Talking about past employment

■ What did you do in Vietnam?
□ I worked in a bank.
■ What kind of work did you do?
□ I was a teller.

■ What did you do in Romania?
□ I worked in a factory.
■ What kind of factory?
□ They made construction equipment.

■ What did you do in Mexico?
□ I was a farmer.
■ What did you raise?
□ Sugar cane.

■ What did you do in Laos?

□ I was a soldier.

■ What kind of work did you do in the army?

□ I was a mechanic.

Practice 1

Read each statement and decide what the next question should be.

Example:

■ *I worked in a hospital.*

□ What kind of work did you do?

1. I was a farmer.
2. I worked in a factory.
3. I was a teacher.
4. I was a soldier.
5. I worked in the refugee camp.

Practice 2

Practice conversations like the following with a partner. Answer about yourself and don't forget to ask your partner about his or her past employment.

■ What did you do in your country?

□ I worked in a hospital.

■ What kind of work did you do?

□ I was a nurse. How about you? What did you do in Mexico?

Practice 3

Write a short conversation like the ones you've been practicing.

■ What did you do in _____?

                                     (your country)

□ _____

■ _____

□ _____

How about you? _____

■ _____

□ _____

■ _____

2. Answering questions about education

- ■ Did you go to school in Cambodia?
- □ Yes, I did.
- ■ How many years did you study?
- □ | For five years.
  | I finished six years of school.
  | I finished high school.
  | I finished two years at the university.

- ■ Did you study English before you came to the U.S.?
- □ Yes, I did.
- ■ How long did you study it?
- □ For three months in Thailand.
- ■ How long have you studied English in the U.S.?
- □ For six months at the International Institute.

Practice

Complete the following conversations about yourself and then practice them with a partner.

1. ■ Did you go to school in _____?
   (your country)

   □ _____

   ■ How many years did you study?

   □ _____

2. ■ Did you study English before you came to the U.S.?

   □ _____

   ■ How long did you study it?

   □ _____

   ■ How long have you studied English in the U.S.?

   □ _____

3. Asking friends what languages they speak

- ■ What languages do you speak?
- □ I know a little Spanish. How about you?
- ■ I only speak English.

Practice

Practice asking a friend what languages he or she speaks.

4. Comparing your new job with your old job

■ Do you like this job better?	☐ Yes. I like the work better, and the pay is better, too.
	Yes. The hours are better here, and the people are friendlier, too.
	No. I don't like the work.
	The pay isn't as good here.
	I don't like the hours.

Practice

The first job is your old job and the second is your new job. The information in parenthesis is about your new job. Practice conversations like the following with your partner.

Example: *salad worker, cook (like work/pay better)*
■ Is this your first job?
☐ No. I was a *salad worker* before.
■ Do you like this job better?
☐ Yes. I *like the work better* and the *pay is better,* too.

1. seamstress, mail worker (like people/pay better)
2. dishwasher, janitor (like work/hours better)
3. secretary, bus driver (like work/pay better)

Role-plays

Student A

1. You and your friend find a place to sit in the lunchroom. You ask your friend where she's from and what she did in her native country.

2. You sit down with your friend at lunch. Ask your friend how much English he has studied in his native country and in the U.S.

3. You and your friend are assemblers. This is your first job in the U.S. Ask your friend if this is her first job and if she likes it better than her other job.

Student B

You sit down with your friend at lunch. You answer questions about working in your native country, and then you ask your friend what he did in his native country.

You sit down with your friend. Answer questions about your study of English. Ask your friend what languages she speaks.

You are an assembler now, but you were a collator before. Your new job pays more and you like the work better. Ask your friend if this is his first job in the U.S.

In the U.S.

Ha Chau came to the United States in 1982. In Vietnam he had worked as a bus driver. When Ha arrived, he studied English for nine months, and then he got a part-time job as a kitchen helper in a restaurant. For three months, Ha worked and studied English. Working as a kitchen helper, Ha didn't make much money, but he got a lot of experience and improved his English. After six months, Ha got a full-time job as a cook in a bigger restaurant. He liked the new job, and the pay was better, too.

Think about these questions:
1. How can a part-time job help you?
2. Why do people change jobs?

Discussing Problems

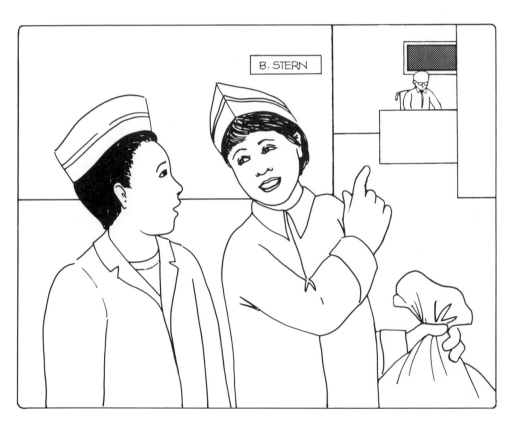

Conversation 1

Som is asking his friend about a problem.

Som: Jim, do you have a minute?

Jim: Sure. What's up?

Som: I want to take an evening class. Who should I talk to about changing my hours?

Jim: Talk to your manager.

Som: Thanks, Jim.

Conversation 2

Later that morning, Som stops his manager in the hall.

Som: Excuse me, Mr. Stern. Could I talk to you a minute?
Manager: I'm sorry, Som. I'm busy right now. How about later this afternoon?
Som: What would be a good time for you, Mr. Stern?
Manager: How about 3:00 in my office?
Som: Good. I'll see you at 3:00 then.

Conversation 3

At 3:00, Som goes to Mr. Stern's office and knocks on the door.

Mr. Stern: Come in and sit down, Som.
Som: Thanks, Mr. Stern.
Mr. Stern: Okay. What can I do for you?
Som: I need to work the day shift on Tuesdays and Thursdays.
Mr. Stern: Why do you want to change shifts now, Som?
Som: I want to take an English class on Tuesday and Thursday evenings.
Mr. Stern: That's a good idea. I'll check, but I think it should be okay.
Som: Thanks a lot, Mr. Stern. I really appreciate it.
Mr. Stern: No problem, Som. I'll get back to you tomorrow, okay?
Som: Good. See you tomorrow then.

Write T for true and F for false.

_____ 1. Som's supervisor can't talk to him in the morning.

_____ 2. Som and his supervisor are going to meet at 2:00 this afternoon.

_____ 3. Som wants to change shifts.

_____ 4. Som wants to work Tuesday and Thursday evenings.

_____ 5. Mr. Stern will tell Som tomorrow if he can change shifts.

Useful Expressions

1. Finding out who to talk to about a problem

■ Who do I talk to about | changing shifts?
taking my vacation?
getting a personal-leave day?
a mistake on my paycheck?
the work schedule?

Practice

Practice finding out who to talk to about a problem. Change the problem each time.

Example: *a mistake on my paycheck*
■ Who do I talk to about *a mistake on my paycheck?*
□ Talk to your supervisor.
■ Thanks.

1. my work schedule
2. changing my hours
3. getting a personal-leave day
4. taking my vacation

2. Arranging to talk to someone

■ Excuse me, Mr. Jones. Could I talk to you a minute?
□ I'm sorry. I'm busy right now.
■ What would be a good time for you?
□ How about tomorrow at 2:00?
■ Okay. See you tomorrow at 2:00.

Practice

Practice conversations like the above with a partner.

3. Stating your problem

■ What can I do for you?
What's the problem?

□ I'd like to | change to the day shift.
have Sundays off.

I think there's | my paycheck.
a mistake on | the work schedule.

I need tomorrow morning off to go to the dentist.

Practice

Read the problem and then practice conversations like the ones above.

Example: *You want to change to the swing shift.*

■ What can I do for you?

□ *I'd like to change to the swing shift.*

1. There's a mistake on your paycheck.
2. You want to have Sundays off instead of Fridays.
3. You want to take your vacation the last week in June.
4. There's a mistake on the work schedule.
5. You need tomorrow afternoon off to go to the dentist.

4. Explaining changes

■ I'd like to change | from the swing shift to the day shift.
| my day off from Friday to Saturday.

I'd like to | work the day shift instead of the swing shift.
| have Saturday off instead of Friday.

Practice

Practice conversations like the ones above. The first time you do the exercise use *change from . . . to* and the second time use *instead of.*

Example:

Your work schedule now	Change you want
Monday off	*Sunday off*

■ I'd like to change from *Monday off* to *Sunday off.*
I'd like *Sunday off* instead of *Monday.*

Your work schedule now	Change you want
1. the swing shift	the day shift
2. Saturday off	Friday off
3. the second shift	the first shift

5. Thanking your boss

■ I'll check on it for you.
That should be okay.
I'll get back to you.

□ I really appreciate it, Mr. Jones.
Thanks. I really appreciate it.

Practice

Write a conversation about a problem you have talked to your boss or supervisor about. Practice the conversation with a partner.

You: *Excuse me.* _____

_____

Supervisor: I'm sorry. I'm busy right now.

You: _____

Supervisor: How about _____

You: _____

You knock on the office door.

Supervisor: Come in.

You: Thanks, _____.
        (supervisor's name)

Supervisor: What can I do for you?

You: _____

Supervisor: I'll check on it and get back to you tomorrow.

You: _____

Role-plays

In these role-plays you are a worker with a problem. Ask a classmate to play the role of your friend. Your teacher or another classmate will be your supervisor. In each role-play, you do three things:

A. Ask a friend who to talk to about your problem.

B. Make an appointment to talk to your supervisor.

C. Talk to your supervisor about the problem.

1. You are working the swing shift now. You want to change to the day shift because your wife just got a job and is working the swing shift too, and there's no one to take care of the children when you are both at work.

2. You think there's a mistake on your paycheck. Usually you get $425 for two weeks, but this pay period you only got $375. You worked the same number of hours both pay periods.

3. You need to take a personal-leave day. On the first of the month, you are moving to a new apartment.

4. You want to change your day off. Now you have Friday and Saturday off. You would like to have Sunday off instead of Friday so you and your wife/husband will have the same day off.

5. You want to take your vacation in July. You would like to take five vacation days starting July 15.

In the U.S.

Lee works in a factory. He has a locker for his things, but no key. He notices that the other workers have keys for their lockers. He is worried that his things will be stolen while he is working. What should Lee do?

Understanding Unions

Unions

In a union, workers join together to improve their wages, hours, working conditions, and job security. Before a union can be started, a majority of the workers must vote to have one.

In some workplaces, both union and non-union workers can be hired; you don't need to be in the union to work. This is called an open shop. At other workplaces, all workers have to join a union or at least pay union dues. This is called a closed shop.

If you are in a union, you must pay dues each month. This money is used by the union to help you. At some workplaces, the dues are deducted from your paycheck; at others, you are responsible for paying your own dues.

Unions help workers in different ways. Here are some examples:

Contracts: One important job unions do is to help workers get good work contracts. A contract is an agreement between management (the employer) and labor (the workers). The contract describes the working hours, wages, and benefits workers will have. It also describes working conditions and grievance procedures (procedures for solving problems at work).

Strikes: Sometimes management and labor cannot agree on a contract. When this happens, workers stop work or go on strike until their employers agree to give them higher pay or better working conditions. During a strike, workers form a picket line to keep non-union workers and customers away from the company. By striking, workers hope to force their employers to sign a fair contract. During the strike, the union helps workers talk to management. They also help workers live during the strike by giving them food and money. When labor and management finally agree and sign a contract, the strike is over, and the workers go back to work.

Grievances: Unions can also help workers solve small problems at work. If a worker has a problem that cannot be solved by talking to a supervisor, he can ask a union representative for help. The union representative will help the worker and the supervisor find an answer to the problem. The pictures below show how a problem can be solved.

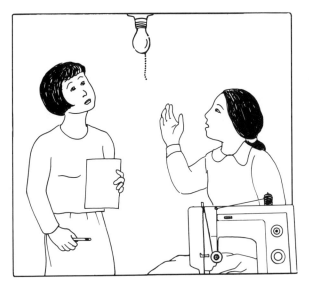

The worker explains the problem to the union representative in her workplace.

The worker and union representative discuss the problem with the employee's supervisor.

The worker and the supervisor come to an agreement and solve the problem.

Write T for true and F for false.

_____ 1. Workers join unions to improve wages, hours, and working conditions.

_____ 2. Workers vote to have a union.

_____ 3. In an open shop, everyone belongs to a union.

_____ 4. In a closed shop, everyone pays union dues.

_____ 5. A strike is when workers stop work because labor and management cannot agree on a contract.

_____ 6. Workers stand in a picket line when they vote for a union.

Practice

Match the term in column B with the appropriate term in column A.

	A		B
_____	1. a complaint or problem		a. management
_____	2. an agreement between employers and workers		b. grievance
_____	3. the employer		c. picket line
_____	4. the worker		d. contract
_____	5. a line of striking workers		e. labor

Using What You Know

If you have been in a union or are in one now, answer the questions about yourself. If you haven't been in a union, interview a union member and then answer the questions.

1. Do you belong to a union? _____ Which union? _____

2. How much are your dues? _____ Are they deducted or do

   you pay them yourself? _____

3. Do you work in an open shop or in a closed shop? _____

   _____

4. Who is your union representative? _____

5. Did you ever bring a problem to your union representative? _____

   What was the problem and what happened? _____

   _____

6. Were you ever in a strike? _____ Did you go on the picket line?

   _____ What was it like? _____

Talking About Coming to the U.S.

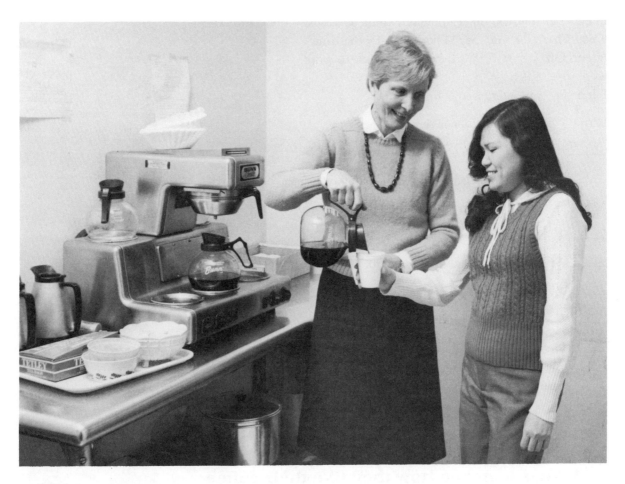

Conversation

Ellen and Keo are getting some coffee before break.

Ellen: Keo, do you use cream and sugar?
Keo: Just a little cream, please.
Ellen: Shall we sit here?
Keo: Sure.
Ellen: This coffee isn't very good, is it?
Keo: It sure isn't.
Ellen: Keo, you're from Laos, right?
Keo: That's right.
Ellen: Why did you leave your country?
Keo: There was a war in Laos. Life was very dangerous.

Ellen: When did you leave?

Keo: In 1978.

Ellen: Did you fly right to the States?

Keo: Oh, no. We walked for many days to get to the Thai border. Then we got a boat across the Mekong River. Many people had to swim, you know.

Ellen: Really?

Keo: Yes. In Thailand, I lived in a refugee camp.

Ellen: How long were you in the camp?

Keo: About a year. In April 1979, I got my papers and flew to the U.S.

Ellen: And how do you like it here?

Keo: I like it, but I miss my country sometimes.

Ellen: I'm sure you do. I know one thing you miss—the warm weather.

Keo: That's for sure. Say, Ellen. What's the time?

Ellen: Oh, it's 3:30. We'd better get back to work.

Keo: Bye, Ellen.

Ellen: See you later, Keo.

Write T for true and F for false.

_____ 1. The coffee isn't good this afternoon.

_____ 2. Life was dangerous in Keo's country.

_____ 3. Keo flew from Laos to the U.S.

_____ 4. Keo had to swim the Mekong.

_____ 5. Keo was in a refugee camp for six months.

_____ 6. Keo misses Laos.

_____ 7. Keo likes the United States.

_____ 8. At 3:30, Keo and Ellen have to go back to work.

Useful Expressions

1. Asking someone how they like their coffee

■ Do you use cream or sugar?

□ A little of both, please.
Just a little cream, please.
A little sugar, please.
No. I drink it black.

2. Talking about the coffee at work

■ This coffee isn't very good.
□ It sure isn't.

■ This coffee is pretty good.
□ It sure is.

Practice

Practice conversations about good and bad coffee with your partner.

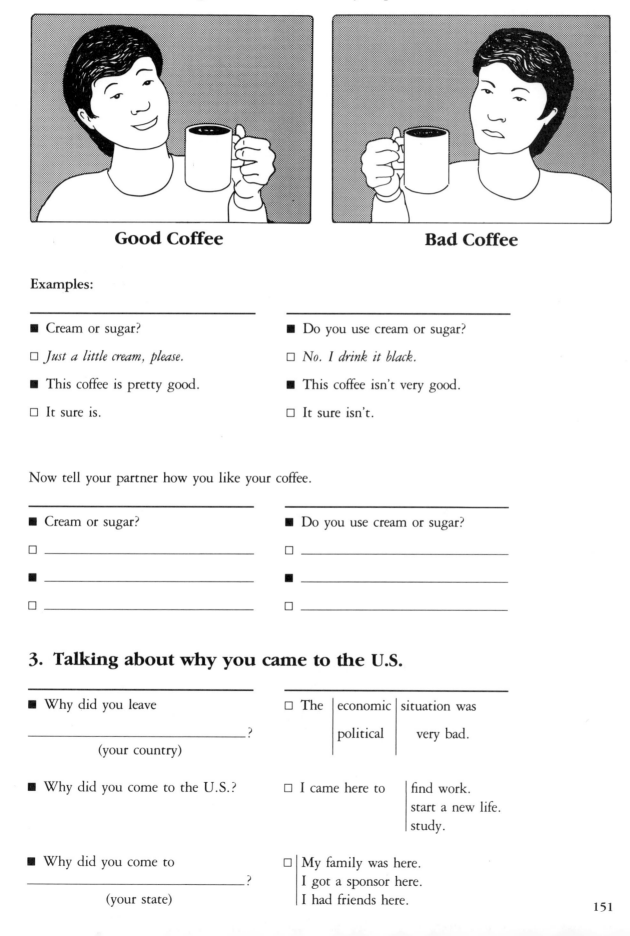

Good Coffee   **Bad Coffee**

Examples:

■ Cream or sugar?

□ *Just a little cream, please.*

■ This coffee is pretty good.

□ It sure is.

■ Do you use cream or sugar?

□ *No. I drink it black.*

■ This coffee isn't very good.

□ It sure isn't.

Now tell your partner how you like your coffee.

■ Cream or sugar?

□ _____

■ _____

□ _____

■ Do you use cream or sugar?

□ _____

■ _____

□ _____

---

3. Talking about why you came to the U.S.

■ Why did you leave

_____ ?
      (your country)

■ Why did you come to the U.S.?

■ Why did you come to

_____ ?
      (your state)

□ The | economic | situation was
      | political | very bad.

□ I came here to | find work.
      | start a new life.
      | study.

□ | My family was here.
  | I got a sponsor here.
  | I had friends here.

151

Practice

First, complete the following conversations with your own answers, and then practice them with a partner until you can say your part without the book.

■ Why did you leave _____?
                    (your country)

□ _____

■ Why did you come to the U.S.?

□ _____

■ Why did you come to _____?
                     (your state)

□ _____

4. Talking about how you left your country

■ How did you leave your country?

□ We left by boat.
            plane.
            car.

□ First we sailed to _____.
      flew

  Then we sailed to the U.S.
       flew

5. Talking about when you left your country

■ When did you leave your country?

□ In 1978.

■ How long were you in the camp?

□ Almost a year.
  A year.
  About two years.

■ When did you come to the States?

□ In 1978.
     April, 1978.

  Seven years ago.

Practice

Write your own answers to these questions and then practice them with your partner.

■ Did you fly right to the U.S.?

□ _____

■ How did you leave your country?

□ _____

■ When did you leave your country?

□ _____

■ How long were you in the camp?

□ _____

■ When did you come to the States?

□ _____

6. Saying you miss your own country

■ How do you like it here?	□	I like it, but I really miss my own country sometimes. I don't like it. I miss _____ _____ too much. (your country)
■ What do you miss the most?	□ I miss my	family. friends.

Practice

Complete the following conversation and then practice it with your partner.

■ How do you like it here?

□ _____

■ What do you miss the most?

□ _____

7. Ending the conversation

■ Say, Ellen. What's the time?
□ It's 3:30 already!
■ We'd better get back to work.
□ Right. Bye, Keo.
■ See you later, Ellen.

Practice

Practice conversations like the one above with a partner.

153

Role-plays

Student A

1. Ask your friend how he wants his coffee. The coffee isn't good. Ask your friend three or four questions about how and why he came to the States. Ask him how he likes the U.S.

2. Ask your friend how she likes her coffee. You say the coffee is good. Answer your friend's questions. Ask what time it is; you have to get back to work.

Student B

You don't like the coffee either. Answer your friend's questions. Ask what time it is; you have to get back to work.

You think the coffee is good, too. Ask your friend three or four questions about how and when she came to the States. Ask what she misses the most.

Using What You've Learned

People will want to know why you left your country and came to the U.S. Write a short paragraph explaining why.

_____

_____

_____

_____

_____

Receiving and Delivering Messages

Conversation 1

Lee is a collator. Beth, her supervisor, needs her to do an errand.

Beth: Lee, I need you to do something for me.
Lee: Okay.
Beth: We're almost out of paper. Could you go to the supply room and ask
  Mrs. Harris to send a number 10 box of white paper?
Lee: A number 10 box?
Beth: Right.
Lee: Okay. I'll go right now.

Answer these questions:

1. Where does Lee have to go?
2. Who does Lee have to talk to?
3. What message does Lee have to give to Mrs. Harris?

Conversation 2

Lee goes to supplies.

Lee: Excuse me. Are you Ms. Harris?

Mrs. Harris: Yes, I am. What can I do for you?

Lee: Beth in collating needs a number 10 box of white paper.

Mrs. Harris: Okay. A number 10 box. I'll send it over by noon.

Lee: Thanks.

Conversation 3

Lee returns to the collating department.

Lee: Excuse me, Beth.

Beth: Yes?

Lee: Ms. Harris will send the paper by noon.

Beth: Oh, that's good. Thanks, Lee.

Lee: You're welcome.

Answer these questions:

1. Does Lee bring a message back to Beth?
2. What is the message for Beth?
3. Who is the second message from?

Useful Expressions

1. Giving messages that request action

■ Could you | tell Ben Lopez to come and fix this machine?
| ask Beth to come to my office at 3:00?
| go to the supply room and ask Mrs. Harris to send a number 10 box of white paper?

■ Please | tell Ken to type this before lunch.
| ask Kevin to redo this letter.
| go to the personnel office and ask John for some time cards.

156

2. Checking that you understand a message

A. Even if you are sure you understand a message, it is a good idea to repeat it.

- ■ Please tell Mrs. Harris to send a number 10 box of white paper.
- ☐ You need a number 10 box of white paper. (statement)
- ■ Right.

B. If you are unsure about part of the message, you can ask a question about it.

- ■ Please tell Mrs. Harris to send a number 10 box of white paper.
- ☐ A number 10 box? (question)
- ■ Right.

Practice

Practice sending messages and checking that you understand them. Tell someone in your class what the message is and who it's for. Also tell your classmate where to deliver the message if necessary. Your partner should check that he/she understands the message as in the examples above. Write the names of your classmates under *Who is the message for?* and begin the practice. The first one has been done below as an example.

- ■ Could you go to personnel and tell Annette to type these letters by 11?
- ☐ You want her to type these letters by 11 o'clock?
  By 11 o'clock?
- ■ Right.

	Where?	Who is the message for?	What is the message?
1.	personnel	*Annette*	type these letters by 11:00
2.	the shop		come and fix this machine before 5:00
3.	the supply room		order three pairs of safety glasses
4.	lunchroom		come to my office during break
5.	packing area		check this time sheet and sign it
6.			

3. Delivering the message and checking back with the sender

A. Sending the message

Bill to **Sarah:** Could you please go to personnel and tell Annette to type these letters by 11:00?

Sarah: You want the letters by 11:00.

Bill: Right.

B. Delivering the message

Sarah to **Annette:** Are you Annette? (If you're not sure who she is.)

Annette: Yes.

Sarah: Bill wants you to type these letters by 11:00.

Annette: Okay. I can do that.

C. Checking back with the sender

Sarah to **Bill:** Excuse me, Bill.

Bill: Yes?

Sarah: Annette says she can do the letters by 11:00.

Bill: That's good. Thanks, Sarah.

Practice

Practice sending and delivering messages and checking back with the sender. Use the messages from the previous practice.

4. Giving messages that request information

Bill to **Ken:** Please ask Victor when he's going on vacation.

Ken: You want to know when he's going on vacation.

Bill: Right.

Ken to **Victor:** Victor, Bill wants to know when you're going on vacation.

Victor: I'm going the second week in July for ten days.

Ken: The second week in July.

Victor: Right.

Ken to **Bill:** Victor's going on vacation the second week in July for ten days.

Bill: Thanks, Ken.

Practice

Write a message with a question and then practice a conversation like the one above with two of your classmates.

_____

_____

_____

_____

Conversation 4

Lee's supervisor, Beth, is busy training some new workers. Lee is answering the phone for her.

Lee: Hello, collating department.
Mr. Smith: I'd like to speak to Beth Johnson, please.
Lee: I'm sorry. She's not in her office right now. Can I take a message?
Mr. Smith: Yes. Would you ask her to call Jim Smith before 5:30 this afternoon.
Lee: Okay. That's Jim Smith. What's your phone number, please?
Mr. Smith: 271-8432.
Lee: That's 271-8432.
Mr. Smith: Right.
Lee: Okay. I'll have her call you, Mr. Smith.
Mr. Smith: Thanks. Good-bye.
Lee: Good-bye.

Write T for true and F for false.

_____ 1. Lee is a receptionist.

_____ 2. Lee is answering the phone for Beth.

_____ 3. Beth can't come to the phone.

_____ 4. Mr. Smith doesn't want to leave a message.

_____ 5. Mr. Smith tells Lee his name and phone number.

_____ 6. Beth will call Mr. Smith later.

Useful Expressions

1. Offering to take a message on the phone

■ Is Ms. Ray there? May I speak to Ms. Ray?	□ I'm sorry. She's not in.	Can I take a message? Do you want to leave a message?

2. Confirming messages

■ Tell her to call Luis Ortega.
□ What's your last name again?
■ Ortega.
□ How do you spell that?
■ O-r-t-e-g-a.
□ O-r-t-e-g-a.

■ My number's 291-7893.
□ What's the number again?
■ 291-7893.
□ 291-7893.
■ That's right.
□ Good. I'll have her call you.

Practice

Practice confirming phone messages. Ask the caller to repeat what is underlined. Practice conversations like this with a partner.

Example: *Jane Green*

■ This is *Jane Green.*
□ What's your last name again?
■ *Green.*
□ How do you spell it?
■ G-r-e-e-n.
□ G-r-e-e-n?
■ That's right.

1. Ben Lopez
2. 221-9779
3. Sarah Black

4. Kim Nguyen
5. 874-8700
6. Henry Frank

Role-plays

In groups of three practice receiving, writing down, and delivering a message.

Example: Anna goes out of the room. Will phones and leaves a message for Anna. Cathy writes down the message for Anna.

Cathy: Hello.
Will: Is Anna there?
Cathy: No, she's out. Can I take a message?
Will: Yes. Tell her to call Will at 645-3573.
(Cathy confirms the message.)
Cathy: I'll have her call you.
Will: Thanks. Good-bye.
Cathy: Bye.

Date ___11/18/85___

Time ___3:00___ AM ☐ PM ☒

To ___Anna___

From ___Will___

Message ___Please call at___

___645-3573.___

___Cathy___
Operator

Anna returns and Cathy delivers the message to her.

Cathy: Will wants you to call him at 645-3573.
Anna: Thanks.

Now you practice. Work in groups of three and use your own names.

Date _____

Time _____ AM ☐ PM ☐

To _____

From _____

Message _____

_____

_____

_____
Operator

Date _____

Time _____ AM ☐ PM ☐

To _____

From _____

Message _____

_____

_____

_____
Operator

W-2 Forms/Paying Taxes

W-2 Forms

Every pay period, your employer withholds (takes out) state and federal taxes from your paycheck. At the end of the year, you receive a W-2 form from your employer which tells you how much money you have earned and how much money has been withheld from your checks. This is important information you will need when you fill out your state and federal tax forms.

Practice

Look at this W-2 form and answer the questions.

1 Control number			
	OMB No. 1545-0008		
2 Employer's name, address, and ZIP code	3 Employer's identification number 41059391	4 Employer's State number 8339390	
St. Paul Company 1300 Como Avenue St. Paul, MN 55108	5 Stat. employee ☐ Deceased ☐ Legal rep. ☐ 942 emp. ☐ Subtotal ☐ Void ☐		
	6 Allocated tips	7 Advance EIC payment .00	
8 Employee's social security number 475-50-3796	9 Federal income tax withheld 1,067.29	10 Wages, tips, other compensation 10,773.00	11 Social security tax withheld 721.71
12 Employee's name, address, and ZIP code	13 Social security wages 10,773.00	14 Social security tips .00	
Jerry Smith 123 Summit Avenue St. Paul, MN 55102	16		
	17 State income tax 555.77	18 State wages, tips, etc. 10,773.00	19 Name of State MN
	20 Local income tax .00	21 Local wages, tips, etc. .00	22 Name of locality

Form **W-2 Wage and Tax Statement**   **1984**   Copy B To be filed with employee's Federal tax return
This information is being furnished to the Internal Revenue Service.   Department of the Treasury Internal Revenue Service

1. How much were Jerry's wages in 1984? _____

2. How much federal income tax was already withheld? _____

3. How much state tax was withheld? _____

4. How much Social Security was withheld? _____

5. What is Jerry's Social Security number? _____

Filling out a tax return

To find out if you owe taxes or if the government owes you a refund, you must fill out a tax return form. The tax form you use depends on your marital status and on the number of deductions you have. The easiest form is the 1040EZ. This form is for single people with no dependents.

Practice

Use the W-2 form in this lesson and complete the following 1040EZ for Jerry Smith. You can put $00.00 on lines 2 and 4 because Jerry has no interest income and has not contributed any money this year. His W-2 form tells you how much federal tax he has already paid. Look at the tax table on page 164 to find out if he still needs to pay more tax or if he should get a refund.

1984 Tax Table

If 1040A, line 19, OR 1040EZ, line 7 is—		And you are—				If 1040A, line 19, OR 1040EZ, line 7 is—		And you are—			
At least	But less than	Single (and 1040EZ filers)	Married filing jointly	Married filing separately	Head of a household	At least	But less than	Single (and 1040EZ filers)	Married filing jointly	Married filing separately	Head of a household
		Your tax is—						Your tax is—			
5,000						**8,000**					
5,000	5,050	329	179	413	306	8,000	8,050	764	543	875	697
5,050	5,100	336	184	420	312	8,050	8,100	771	550	884	704
5,100	5,150	343	190	427	318	8,100	8,150	779	557	893	711
5,150	5,200	350	195	434	324	8,150	8,200	786	564	902	718
5,200	5,250	357	201	441	330	8,200	8,250	794	571	911	725
5,250	5,300	364	206	448	336	8,250	8,300	801	578	920	732
5,300	5,350	371	212	455	342	8,300	8,350	809	585	929	739
5,350	5,400	378	217	462	348	8,350	8,400	816	592	938	746
5,400	5,450	385	223	469	354	8,400	8,450	824	599	947	753
5,450	5,500	392	228	476	360	8,450	8,500	831	606	956	760
5,500	5,550	399	234	483	366	8,500	8,550	839	613	965	767
5,550	5,600	406	240	490	372	8,550	8,600	847	620	974	774
5,600	5,650	413	246	497	378	8,600	8,650	855	627	983	781
5,650	5,700	420	252	504	384	8,650	8,700	863	634	992	788
5,700	5,750	427	258	511	390	8,700	8,750	871	641	1,001	795
5,750	5,800	434	264	518	396	8,750	8,800	879	648	1,010	804
5,800	5,850	441	270	525	402	8,800	8,850	887	655	1,019	812
5,850	5,900	448	276	532	408	8,850	8,900	895	662	1,028	821
5,900	5,950	455	282	539	414	8,900	8,950	903	669	1,037	829
5,950	6,000	462	288	547	420	8,950	9,000	911	676	1,046	838
6,000						**9,000**					
6,000	6,050	469	294	555	426	9,000	9,050	919	683	1,055	846
6,050	6,100	476	300	563	432	9,050	9,100	927	690	1,064	855
6,100	6,150	483	306	571	438	9,100	9,150	935	697	1,073	863
6,150	6,200	490	312	579	444	9,150	9,200	943	704	1,082	872
6,200	6,250	497	318	587	450	9,200	9,250	951	711	1,091	880
6,250	6,300	504	324	595	456	9,250	9,300	959	718	1,100	889
6,300	6,350	511	330	603	462	9,300	9,350	967	725	1,109	897
6,350	6,400	518	336	611	468	9,350	9,400	975	732	1,118	906
6,400	6,450	525	342	619	474	9,400	9,450	983	739	1,127	914
6,450	6,500	532	348	627	480	9,450	9,500	991	746	1,136	923
6,500	6,550	539	354	635	487	9,500	9,550	999	753	1,145	931
6,550	6,600	546	360	643	494	9,550	9,600	1,007	760	1,154	940
6,600	6,650	554	366	651	501	9,600	9,650	1,015	767	1,163	948
6,650	6,700	561	372	659	508	9,650	9,700	1,023	774	1,172	957
6,700	6,750	569	378	667	515	9,700	9,750	1,031	781	1,181	965
6,750	6,800	576	384	675	522	9,750	9,800	1,039	788	1,190	974
6,800	6,850	584	390	683	529	9,800	9,850	1,047	795	1,199	982
6,850	6,900	591	396	691	536	9,850	9,900	1,055	802	1,208	991
6,900	6,950	599	402	699	543	9,900	9,950	1,063	809	1,217	999
6,950	7,000	606	408	707	550	9,950	10,000	1,071	816	1,226	1,008
7,000						**10,000**					
7,000	7,050	614	414	715	557	10,000	10,050	1,079	823	1,235	1,016
7,050	7,100	621	420	723	564	10,050	10,100	1,087	830	1,244	1,025
7,100	7,150	629	426	731	571	10,100	10,150	1,095	837	1,254	1,033
7,150	7,200	636	432	739	578	10,150	10,200	1,103	844	1,265	1,042
7,200	7,250	644	438	747	585	10,200	10,250	1,111	851	1,276	1,050
7,250	7,300	651	444	755	592	10,250	10,300	1,119	858	1,287	1,059
7,300	7,350	659	450	763	599	10,300	10,350	1,127	865	1,298	1,067
7,350	7,400	666	456	771	606	10,350	10,400	1,135	872	1,309	1,076
7,400	7,450	674	462	779	613	10,400	10,450	1,143	879	1,320	1,084
7,450	7,500	681	468	787	620	10,450	10,500	1,151	886	1,331	1,093
7,500	7,550	689	474	795	627	10,500	10,550	1,159	893	1,342	1,101
7,550	7,600	696	480	803	634	10,550	10,600	1,167	900	1,353	1,110
7,600	7,650	704	487	811	641	10,600	10,650	1,175	907	1,364	1,118
7,650	7,700	711	494	819	648	10,650	10,700	1,183	914	1,375	1,127
7,700	7,750	719	501	827	655	10,700	10,750	1,191	921	1,386	1,135
7,750	7,800	726	508	835	662	10,750	10,800	1,199	928	1,397	1,144

Department of the Treasury - Internal Revenue Service

Form 1040EZ Income Tax Return for
Single filers with no dependents

1984

OMB No. 1545-0675

Name & address	Use the IRS mailing label. If you don't have one, please print: Print your name above (first, initial, last) Present home address (number and street) City, town, or post office, State, and ZIP code

Please print your numbers like this.

$\fbox{1}\fbox{2}\fbox{3}\fbox{4}\fbox{5}\fbox{6}\fbox{7}\fbox{8}\fbox{9}\fbox{0}$

Social security number

Presidential Election Campaign Fund
Check box if you want $1 of your tax to go to this fund. ▶

Dollars   Cents

Figure your tax

1 Total wages, salaries, and tips. This should be shown in Box 10 of your W-2 form(s). (Attach your W-2 form(s).)   **1**

2 Interest income of $400 or less. If the total is more than $400, you cannot use Form 1040EZ.   **2**

Attach Copy B of Form(s) W-2 here

3 Add line 1 and line 2. This is your **adjusted gross income.**   **3**

4 Allowable part of your charitable contributions. Complete the worksheet on page 21 of the instruction booklet. Do not enter more than $75.   **4**

5 Subtract line 4 from line 3.   **5**

6 Amount of your personal exemption.   **6** $1,000.00$

7 Subtract line 6 from line 5. This is your **taxable income.**   **7**

8 Enter your Federal income tax withheld. This should be shown in Box 9 of your W-2 form(s).   **8**

9 Use the **single** column in the tax table on pages 31-36 of the instruction booklet to find the **tax** on your taxable income on line 7. Enter the amount of tax.   **9**

Refund or amount you owe

10 If line 8 is larger than line 9, subtract line 9 from line 8. Enter the **amount of your refund.**   **10**

11 If line 9 is larger than line 8, subtract line 8 from line 9. Enter the **amount you owe.** Attach check or money order for the full amount, payable to "Internal Revenue Service."   **11**

Attach tax payment here

Sign your return

I have read this return. Under penalties of perjury, I declare that to the best of my knowledge and belief, the return is true, correct, and complete.

Your signature   Date

For IRS Use Only — Please do not write in boxes below.

For **Privacy Act and Paperwork Reduction Act Notice, see page 41.**

Tax Return Help: Because filling out tax returns is not easy, many people get someone to help them prepare (fill out) their tax forms. If you need help, ask a friend to recommend someone or look under "Tax Return Preparation" in the yellow pages of your phone book.

Making Friends

Conversation

Luis is looking for a place to sit down and have lunch.

Luis: Is this place taken?
Chuck: No. Go ahead and sit down.
Luis: Thanks. I'm Luis Torres. I work in packing.
Chuck: Nice to meet you, Luis. I'm Chuck Baker.
Luis: Nice to meet you, Chuck.
Chuck: And this is my friend, Al.
Luis: Nice to meet you, Al.
Al: Same here, Luis.
Chuck: Did you see the Twins play last night?
Luis: No, I didn't. Who won?

Al: The Twins—9 to 5.
Chuck: Do they play much baseball in your country?
Luis: Some, but soccer is the most popular game in Mexico.
Al: Soccer's getting popular in the U.S., too.
Luis: Yeah, I know. I play on a team here.
Chuck: Excuse me. I have to get back to work. Nice to meet you, Luis.
Luis: Nice meeting you, Chuck.
Al: I have to get back, too. Nice meeting you, Luis.
Luis: Same here, Al.

Write T for true and F for false.

_____ 1. Luis sits next to some friends.

_____ 2. Chuck introduces Luis to his friend Al.

_____ 3. The men are talking about baseball.

_____ 4. Luis didn't see the baseball game.

_____ 5. They don't play baseball in Mexico.

_____ 6. Soccer is getting popular in the U.S.

Useful Expressions

1. Finding a place to sit down

■ Is this chair taken?
□ No. Go ahead and sit down.
■ Thanks.

■ Is this place free?
□ Sure. Have a seat.
■ Thanks.

■ Is this chair taken?
□ Sorry, it is.
■ Thanks anyway.

2. Introductions

A. Introducing yourself
Khoa: Hello, my name's Khoa Pham.
John: Nice to meet you, Khoa. I'm John Smith.
Khoa: Nice to meet you, John.

B. Introducing others
John: Khoa this is my friend André.
Khoa: Nice to meet you, André.
André: Nice to meet you too, Khoa.

C. Saying good-bye to people you have just met

André: I have to get back to work. Nice to have met you, Khoa.

Khoa: Nice meeting you too, André.

Practice

Practice introducing yourself and others. Follow the examples above.

3. Talking about sports

- Did you see the Twins play last night?
- □ Yes, I did. They looked bad.
- What was the score?
- □ The Twins lost 14 to 8.

- Did you see the Vikings play yesterday?
- □ Yes, I saw the game on TV. They really looked good.
- Who won?
- □ The Vikings won 13 to 7.

- Did you see the soccer game last night?
- □ No, I missed it. What was the score?
- Our team won 5 to 4.
- □ That was close.

Practice

Have conversations with your partner about the sports teams below.

Example

team	score
Twins	7
White Sox	11

- Did you see the Twins game yesterday?
- □ Yes, I did. They really looked bad.
- Who won?
- □ The White Sox—11 to 7.

	team	score
1.	Vikings	14
	Rams	7
2.	Kicks	4
	Cosmos	5

4. Answering questions about sports

■ Do they play much baseball in your country?

□ No, they don't.

■ What sports are popular there?

□ Soccer is popular and volleyball is, too.

■ Is baseball popular in Mexico?

□ Yes, it's very popular.

Practice

Talk with your partner about sports in his/her country. Follow these examples:

Example: *baseball* | *in* _____

(partner's country)

■ Do they play much *baseball in Laos?*

□ No, they don't.

■ What sports are popular there?

□ Soccer is popular and volleyball is, too.

■ Is *baseball* popular *in Japan?*

□ Yes, it's very popular.

1. hockey | in _____
2. soccer | (your partner's country)
3. football
4. volleyball
5. basketball
6. baseball

Role-plays

Student A

1. You ask if you can sit down. You introduce yourself and say what department you're in. B asks you about sports in your country. You answer. You ask if soccer is popular in her country.

Student B

The chair next to you is free. You are happy to meet A. You ask A what sports are popular in his country. At 3:30 you say that you have to get back to work.

Now work in groups of three.

Student A

2. You ask B if you can sit down, then you introduce yourself. You didn't see the game. You ask about the score.

Student B

The chair is free. You are happy to meet A. You introduce your friend C. You ask A if she saw the soccer game last night. The score was 5 to 4.

Student C

You are happy to meet A. You listen for a few minutes, then you say that you have to get back to work.

168

Talking About Advancement

Conversation 1

Carmen is talking to her supervisor about changing to a new job in her company.

Supervisor: Come in and sit down, Carmen.
Carmen: Thanks.
Supervisor: What can I do for you?
Carmen: I'd like to talk to you about job advancement.
Supervisor: What do you want to know?
Carmen: Well, are there other jobs I could apply for in the company?
Supervisor: What's your job now?
Carmen: I fold towels in the laundry department.
Supervisor: How long have you had that job?
Carmen: About a year.
Supervisor: Okay. There are some other jobs in the laundry department. You could apply to be a dryer operator.
Carmen: What are the duties?
Supervisor: You have to operate the dryers, load and unload the dryers, and deliver the clothes to folding.
Carmen: How would I learn the job?
Supervisor: Another worker will train you.
Carmen: I see. And how do I apply?
Supervisor: Check the job postings and sign your name by the job you want.
Carmen: Thanks for your help, Robert.
Supervisor: You're welcome. Good-bye, Carmen.

Write T for true and F for false.

_____ 1. Carmen wants to change jobs at her company.

_____ 2. She is talking to her supervisor.

_____ 3. Carmen has worked folding towels for one year.

_____ 4. She is a dryer operator now.

_____ 5. The dryer operator has to deliver the clothes to folding.

_____ 6. Carmen will learn her new job from her supervisor.

_____ 7. Carmen can apply for a job by signing her name next to the job she wants.

Useful Expressions

1. Asking about job advancement

■ I'd like to talk to you about job advancement.
□ What do you want to know?
■ Are there other jobs I could apply for in the company?

Practice

Practice saying the above conversation with your partner.

2. Answering questions about your job

■ What are you doing now? What's your job now?	□ I fold towels in the laundry department.
■ How long have you been doing that job?	□ (For) about ■ a year. two years.

3. Talking about job duties

■ You could apply to be a dryer operator.
□ What are the job duties?
■ You operate the dryers, load and unload the dryers, and deliver the clothes to folding.
□ How would I learn to operate the dryers?
■ Another worker will train you.

Practice

If you are working, fill in the blanks below, describing the duties of your present job. Then describe the duties of a job you would like to do.

Your present job: _____

How long have you had this job? _____

The job you would like: _____

Duties of that job: _____

_____

Now practice this conversation with your teacher or another student, using the information you have just written down.

Supervisor: What can I do for you?

Worker: I'd like to talk to you about _____.

Supervisor: What do you want to know?

Worker: _____

Supervisor: What's your job now?

Worker: _____

Supervisor: How long have you been doing that job?

Worker: _____

Supervisor: You could apply to be a _____.
                                        (new job)

Worker: _____ duties?

Supervisor: You have to _____

_____.

Worker: How _____?

Supervisor: Another worker will train you.

```
┌─────────────────────────────────────────────────────────┐
│              ┌───────────────────────────┐               │
│              │  EMPLOYMENT ANNOUNCEMENTS │               │
│              └───────────────────────────┘               │
│  ┌──────────────────────┐    ┌──────────────────────┐    │
│  │ LAUNDRY DEPARTMENT   │    │ HOUSEKEEPING         │    │
│  │                      │    │                      │    │
│  │ Job:  Dryer operator │    │ Job:  Janitor        │    │
│  │                      │    │                      │    │
│  │ Duties:  Load and    │    │ Duties:  Clean and   │    │
│  │   unload dryers;     │    │   wax floors;        │    │
│  │   deliver clothes    │    │   clean windows      │    │
│  │   to folding.        │    │   and walls.         │    │
│  │                      │    │                      │    │
│  │ Requirements: Must   │    │ Requirements: Must   │    │
│  │   be able to do      │    │   be able to use     │    │
│  │   strenuous work.    │    │   electric waxing    │    │
│  │                      │    │   equipment.         │    │
│  │ Hours: 7 a.m. to     │    │ Hours: 4:30 p.m. to  │    │
│  │   3:30 p.m.          │    │   12:30 a.m.         │    │
│  │                      │    │                      │    │
│  │ Pay: $6.50 an hour   │    │ Pay: $6.00 an hour   │    │
│  │                      │    │                      │    │
│  │ Available: Immediate │    │ Available:           │    │
│  │   opening            │    │   Immediately        │    │
│  │                      │    │                      │    │
│  │ 1. Chi Qui           │    │ 1. Mike Brown        │    │
│  │ 2. Joan Hill         │    │ 2.                   │    │
│  │ 3. Carmen Diaz       │    │ 3.                   │    │
│  └──────────────────────┘    └──────────────────────┘    │
└─────────────────────────────────────────────────────────┘
```

Conversation 2

After talking to her supervisor, Carmen signed up for the dryer operator job. A week later, she is called in for an interview. She knocks on the personnel manager's door.

Mrs. Olson: Come in. Please sit down, Carmen.

Carmen: Thank you, Mrs. Olson.

Mrs. Olson: What job are you applying for?

Carmen: Dryer Operator.

Mrs. Olson: Do you understand the duties?

Carmen: Yes. I have to load and unload the dryers and deliver the clothes to folding.

Mrs. Olson: This is heavy work, you know.

Carmen: Yes, I know, but I can handle it.

Mrs. Olson: Okay, Carmen. You have the seniority and I know you can do the job. You can start on the 15th. Do you understand probation?

Carmen: I think so. I have thirty days to learn the job, right?

Mrs. Olson: Yes, that's right. Do you have any questions?

Carmen: No, I don't think so.

Mrs. Olson: Well, good luck, Carmen.

Carmen: Thanks, Mrs. Olson. Have a good day.

Mrs. Olson: You too.

Answer these questions about the conversation:

_____ 1. Carmen is applying for the dryer operator job.

_____ 2. She is talking to the personnel manager.

_____ 3. Carmen doesn't understand the job duties.

_____ 4. She can handle heavy work.

_____ 5. Carmen doesn't have seniority.

_____ 6. She has 30 days to learn her new job.

_____ 7. Carmen got the job.

Useful Expressions

1. Stating what job you're applying for

■ What job are you applying for?	□ Receptionist. The receptionist job.

Practice

Practice conversations like the following with your partner.

Examples:

receptionist
■ What job are you applying for?
□ *Receptionist.*
   The *receptionist* job.

typist/typing
■ What job are you applying for?
□ *Typist.*
   The *typing* job.

1. receptionist
2. kitchen helper
3. machinist
4. typist/typing

5. packer/packing
6. housekeeper/housekeeping
7. janitor/janitorial
8. secretary/secretarial

2. Describing job duties

■ Do you understand the job duties?	□ Yes. I have to type, file, and answer phones.

Practice

Write down two jobs and the duties for each job, and then practice the following conversation. Choose jobs that you have had or would like to have.

Job: _____ Job: _____

Job duties: _____ Job duties: _____

_____ _____

_____ _____

■ What job are you applying for?
□ I'm applying for the secretarial job.
■ Do you understand what the job duties are?
□ Yes. I have to type, file, and answer the phone.

3. Being positive about your abilities

■ Do you think you can learn this job?	□ Yes.	I'm sure I can. I know I can. I'll really try hard to learn it.
■ Do you know how to operate the washers?	□ No, but I'm sure I can learn.	
■ Is your English good enough?	□ I hope so. I'm studying English at night.	
■ Is your typing good enough?	□ Yes. I can type 50 words per minute.	
■ Are you strong enough to do this work?	□ Yes.	I can handle it. I'm very strong.
■ Can you read well enough?	□ Yes, I'm sure I can.	

Practice

Practice answering positively about your abilities. How would you respond to
each of these questions?

Example:

■ Can you learn this job?

□ Yes. I know I can.

1. Is your English good enough?
2. Do you think you can learn to operate the dryers?
3. Are you strong enough to do this work?
4. Is your typing good enough?
5. Can you do filing?
6. Can you read well enough to do the job?
7. Can you fix foreign cars?

Role-plays

Complete the following job announcement and then practice a job interview with
your teacher.

(Department)

Job: _____

Duties: _____

_____

Requirements: _____

_____

Hours: _____

Pay: _____

Available: _____

Understanding Job Posting

Job Posting

Why change your job? There are two or three main reasons why people change jobs. Can you think of some?

1. _____

2. _____

3. _____

At most workplaces, available jobs are first offered to people who already work for the company. In this lesson, you will learn how to find out about available jobs and how to apply for them.

Posting or announcing the job: When a job becomes available, the company puts up (posts) a notice announcing the job opening. As you saw in Section 2 of this Unit, workers show that they want to apply for a posted job by signing their name under the job or by telling their supervisor or personnel manager that they are interested in the opening.

Practice

Here are some sample job postings. As you answer the following questions, pay attention to the information that is usually given in a job announcement.

```
FOOD SERVICE

Job:  Kitchen helper

Duties:  Load and unload dishwasher,
         help in food preparation.

Demands:  Must be able to do
          heavy work.

Hours:  Part-time; 1-5 p.m.

Pay:  $4.00 an hour

Available:  Start June 15

_____

_____

_____
```

```
CLERICAL DEPARTMENT

Job:  Secretary

Duties:  Type, file, and answer
         phones.

Demands:  Must be able to type
          45 w.p.m.

Hours:  8 a.m. to 5 p.m.

Pay:  $4.50 an hour

Available:  Start June 1

_____

_____

_____
```

1. What job is available in the Food Service Department?
2. When is the job available?
3. What are the hours?
4. Is the work heavy or light?
5. How much is the pay?
6. What are the job duties?
7. What job is available in the Clerical Department?
8. Is this job for the day shift or for the night shift?
9. Does the job have any special demands?
10. What are the job duties?
11. When is the job available?
12. What is the pay for the secretarial job?

Advancement

Interviewing for the job: Each person who has shown an interest in the job will be interviewed. The interviewer needs to find out which worker can do the best job. The worker must be able to meet the job demands and be able to learn the new job easily. In some companies, especially if there is a union, the interviewer also needs to know which worker has the highest seniority, that is, which worker has worked at the company the longest. If two workers have the same qualifications, the worker who has worked the longest will usually get the new job.

Probation period: A probation period is the time a worker has to show that he can learn his new job. Usually the worker learns his job from the person who is leaving it. If a worker can't learn the new job during the probation period, he is usually allowed to go back to his old job; he is not fired.

The worker's responsibility: If you want to change jobs, it is your responsibility to check for job postings. If you don't understand how job posting works at your company, you should ask your supervisor or personnel manager.

Write T for true and F for false.

_____ 1. Workers usually change jobs because they want better pay or because they like the new job better.

_____ 2. Announcements for jobs are usually posted on a bulletin board at the workplace.

_____ 3. Supervisors are happy to explain job announcements if workers ask them.

_____ 4. Job announcements usually tell you what the hours are for a job.

_____ 5. If the work is heavy, you should apply only if you are very strong.

_____ 6. Workers with the highest seniority usually get the job if they can meet the job demands.

_____ 7. You must know exactly how to do a job before you start.

_____ 8. Workers show they can do their new job during the probation period.

_____ 9. If a worker doesn't learn the new job during the probation period, he is usually fired.

_____ 10. *Available immediately* means that a worker is needed for a job right now.

Using What You've Learned

If you are working, bring in some examples of job announcements from your workplace. Also be prepared to explain how job posting works at your company.